REVELATION RIDDLE: KINGDOM AGE OF THE SAINTS

End Times for the New World Order

Benjamin Thomas

REVELATION RIDDLE: KINGDOM AGE OF THE SAINTS
END TIMES FOR THE NEW WORLD ORDER

Copyright © 2023 by Gloriam Media LLC

No part of this book may be reproduced or transmitted in any form or by any means whatsoever including photocopying, scanning, digitizing, recording, or any form of information storage and retrieval system, without written permission from the author or his heirs with the exception of brief quotations in articles or reviews.

While every effort has been made to ensure the accuracy and effectiveness of the information in this book the author makes no guarantee, express or implied, as to the procedures contained herein. Neither the author nor the publisher will be liable for direct, incidental, or consequential damages in connection with or arising from the furnishing, performance, or use of this book.

Scripture quotations marked KJV are taken from the King James Version of the Holy Bible (Public Domain). Scripture quotations marked YLT are taken from the Youngs Literal Translation of the Holy Bible (Public Domain).

Scripture quotations marked ASV are taken from the American Standard Version of the Holy Bible (Public Domain).

Scripture quotations marked Darby are taken from the Darby Translation Bible (Public Domain).

Scripture quotations marked NKJV are taken from the New King James Version®. Copyright © 1982 by Thomas Nelson. Used by permission. All rights reserved.

Scripture quotations marked CEV are from the Contemporary English Version Copyright © 1991, 1992, 1995 by American Bible Society. Used by Permission.

Scripture quotations marked NCV are taken from the New Century Version® of the Holy Bible. Copyright © 2005 by Thomas Nelson. Used by permission. All rights reserved.

Scripture quotations marked AMPC are taken from the Amplified® Bible, Copyright © 1954, 1958, 1962, 1964, 1965, 1987 by The Lockman Foundation. Used by permission. lockman.org.

Scripture quotations marked NLT are taken from the Holy Bible, New Living Translation, Copyright ©1996, 2004, 2015 by Tyndale House Foundation. Used by permission of Tyndale House Publishers, Carol Stream, Illinois 60188. All rights reserved.

Scripture quotations marked MSG are taken from The Message, Copyright © 1993, 2002, 2018 by Eugene H. Peterson. Used by permission of NavPress. All rights reserved. Represented by Tyndale House Publishers.

All emphasis in Scripture quotations is added by the author.

ISBN: 979-8-9892115-0-0 (eBook)
ISBN: 979-8-9892115-1-7 (Paperback)
ISBN: 979-8-9892115-5-5 (Hardcover)
ISBN: 979-8-9892115-2-4 (Audio)

Cover by SN

Illustrations by Michael W.

First edition: January 2024 Rev.

Dedicated to Mom,
who never stopped praying for me.

Those who hear and don't act are like those who glance in the mirror, walk away, and two minutes later have no idea who they are, what they look like.

– James 1:23-24 MSG

CONTENTS

My Story 1
1. Something is Wrong 5
2. The Church Paralyzed 13
3. Intelligence Briefing on Our Enemy 23
4. Butchers in Suits And Gowns 47
5. Learning to Fight Back 75
6. The Death of the Fourth Beast 93
7. Dominion Transfer to the Saints 119
8. Treasure in Fallen Fortresses 135
9. The Revelation Riddle 151
10. The World Under the Saints 163
11. The Rapture and the Dragon 179
12. Prepare, Soldier Saints! 191
Appendix
Don't Wait, Receive Jesus Today! 207

My Story

I grew up in a broken home. My parents piled up eight marriages between them. Although I was raised as a Christian, the divorce of my parents when I was twelve years old caused me to run from God. In junior high, my teachers sent me to a counselor weekly to help me with depression. After several years of rebellion, God drew me back to Himself in college. I fell in love with the Bible, literally wearing out several Bibles while also studying for a science degree. Just prior to my return to God, the wildest fraternity on campus recruited me to join them, but I realized I could not serve God and chase girls at the same time. After I fell in love with God, I completely pulled away from partying, and my pledge class thought I was totally crazy. I soon found myself with few friends my own age in college.

God had radically transformed me. Witnessing at the edge of the quadrangle on campus to college students proved to be over-the-top even for the local Bible study kids. I did have one adult pastor friend, and we marched around campus together many times, praying for revival. We ran a weekly live worship service every Friday night for a couple of years in the campus chapel. Unfortunately, we lost access to the chapel after we sponsored an event for Jews for Jesus on campus, infuriating the local Chabad house.

I began to learn to trust God like a child. I remember reading Mark 16:18 (AMPC) during my college studies: "They will lay hands on the sick, and they will get well." Upon reading this scripture, I immediately went out to test it; I would find any person with a sniffle and offer to pray for them. I saw many miracles while I was still in college and witnessed additional miracles after graduation as I spoke to storms and continued to pray for the sick. Another miracle I experienced while in college involved provision.

Each semester could have been my last due to lack of finances. My parents could not help me financially and my campus job did not cover attending one of the most expensive schools in the United States. Each month, I would bring my bills to God, and say, "Daddy, this one's for you!" God always provided in unusual ways. Somehow, I lived rent-free for two of my four years during college. In one instance, my landlord never paid the electric bill and felt guilty that there was no hot water, so he never asked me for rent! I powered my computer with an extension cord to the neighbor's in order to get my homework done. I graduated college as many do – ready to change the world. However, because I had witnessed God working miraculously so many times, I knew my journey would not be ordinary.

Fast-forward a couple of years and I was commuting on a bus into New York City from New Jersey, excited to work another day on my new company, which attracted a mere $30,000 of initial investment capital. I lived in my investor's basement in New Jersey. My lunch budget at the time amounted to $3, made possible by hot dog stands. Utterly naive but believing God had called me to the business world, I went after the American Dream. I would arrive in Midtown Manhattan and, standing on a street corner, shout at the skyline: "New York City, you love my ideas and are investing in them. Capital, people, and resources are coming my way, in Jesus' name!" Well, it happened! In my early twenties, with the help of investors, I bought a company for $60 million, which in a few years sold for nearly $200 million. I went on to buy over thirty companies through various businesses. Along the way, I worked with great people. I also attracted really evil people. I survived two hostile takeover attempts, one of which nearly wiped me out. I learned the hard way that debt financing is great...until it isn't.

A few years ago, a buddy of mine from New York visited me and shared a bunch of what seemed like wacko stories about central banks actually being private and how the world was in reality controlled by just a handful of powerful families. I had just seen *The Matrix* movie and my friend's stories sounded like science fiction fantasy. After doing my own research, I realized my friend was right.

For a couple of years, I fell into a funk. I recognized that all my assumptions about how the world worked were wrong; the way the system really worked scared the hell out of me. I became far more interested in End Times teaching than ever before; however, it seemed like most Christian teaching could by summarized by: "Oh yeah, the world gets really bad, but then Jesus rescues us just before we get killed by the anti-Christ." Becoming more and more fearful, I became a prepper, building out escape vehicles and planning exit routes for when the crap hit the fan. This took a toll on me financially, and my family thought I was nuts. Worse, I could not get a clear answer from God and felt fear drawing me away from Him.

At my lowest point, I began to seek God about what the Bible actually said about the end of the world. Something in me did not agree with the Church teaching that God had planned an escape hatch for His people to flee from Satan. Satan never had the upper hand in the Bible. Something seemed very wrong not only with the world but also with the Church. The Church even seemed to be okay with Satan running roughshod on just about everyone, totally apathetic as establishment institutions suffered infiltration. Worse, I found many churches apparently in on the corruption, particularly concerning child trafficking. I wondered, where were the Joshuas of our day?

It frustrated me to sit and look at the Bible on my desk, knowing the answers were in there somewhere. Finally I asked God to show me where to look. What I discovered in the Bible blew me away. Not only was God's plan better than anything than I heard from any pastor, but God's plan aligned with how He had operated in the past when dealing with Babel, Egypt, and other world powers. God does not run from anything – He is total victory.

I am going to show you God's plan for our future – it's far better than anything you have been taught. In fact, now is the best time to be alive since Jesus came. I am going to blow the whistle on how Satan infiltrated and perverted faith and governments to reach his objective of world control. Once your eyes are opened, you will operate at a level you never thought possible. Your knowledge of what's coming will set you free from fear and anxiety. You will see through the matrix and walk at a level of hope you never thought possible as you watch your dreams come back to life and accelerate. You will develop your skills as a Soldier Saint.

It's the End Times for the New World Order as we transition to the Kingdom Age of the Saints. We are not enduring the Great Tribulation, neither are we in the battle of Armageddon. It's resume time as God recruits saints to lead the world after the largest wealth transfer in history – even bigger than the Exodus of Israel from Egypt. The choice is yours – get in the fight and plunder the spoils or continue to hide and wait for a rescue rapture that's not coming.

All is about to change. The planet will soon reboot with a completely different operating system. It's time for the saints to rise up and lead. God is calling you to rise up as a Soldier Saint in the new age. Will you accept the call?

1. Something is Wrong

Hooray! Hooray! The end of the world has been postponed!
– Hergé, The Shooting Star

Something is wrong with our world – people sense it. Broken, violated, and stayed appears the spiritual law of the harvest for evil perpetrators. The unholy alliance between Big Government and Big Corporations wreaks havoc on civil society, now desperate to find footing. Many freedom lovers, deflated and forsaken by unreliable and rigged justice systems, are tempted to give up.

Religious institutions are utterly powerless in the face of the evil march of the world system. A few pastors here and there are standing up, but for the most part, the Church appears to be a toothless tiger. Many church members quietly sit behind-the-scenes and hope no one from the government knocks on their door. Most believe a rapture is coming to rescue God's people. Surveys indicate that, particularly in America, we are losing our faith. Where is God in all this?

Hollywood fills the void by providing a steady stream of entertaining apocalyptic movies. *Resident Evil,* starring Milla Jovovich, remains a personal favorite. In the *Resident Evil* movie series, a corporation globally known for household and pharmaceutical products experiments in a lab with viruses.[1] The research spirals out of control when the leaked virus transforms humans into flesh-eating zombies. The company profits from the deadly T-virus with government contracts. Late in the series, viewers learn the evil corporation intentionally released the virus to destroy humanity before, in their opinion, humanity would destroy itself. Alice, the protagonist, fights zombies and attempts to topple the evil corporation but not before the entire world is reduced to dust and populated by roaming, hungry, disfigured walking dead.

The End Makes for a Great Story

Hundreds of apocalyptic movies came out over the last few decades.[2] In the *Left Behind* movie series, starring Kirk Cameron, Christians portray their version of the end. A mysterious event occurs, causing millions of Christian believers to disappear, leaving the world in dark disarray. Airplanes flown by Christian pilots crash, families are confused, and a small band of believers emerges to evangelize remaining society, now enduring a brutal anti-Christ dictator rapidly consolidating power. A secular version depicting the Rapture starred Nicholas Cage. My curiosity regarding how others believe the world

---

[1] *Resident Evil*, dir. Paul W. S. Anderson, prod. Bernd Eichinger, Samuel Hadida, Jeremy Bolt & Paul W. S. Anderson, 2002
[2] "List of apocalyptic films," accessed May 11, 2023, *Wikipedia.org*, https://en.wikipedia.org/wiki/List_of_apocalyptic_films.

ends continues to draw me to apocalyptic films. The smallest details interest me. In a recent apocalyptic film, the main character escaped world destruction by driving an older model Jeep Wagoneer – a model without electronic ignition.

Plots of secular apocalyptic films follow predictable story lines:

1. Aliens invade and exterminate humanity.
2. A manmade deadly disease wipes out all the people.
3. A natural disaster or large asteroid destroys much of the earth.
4. Extreme famine or human sterility causes masses to die off.
5. Artificial intelligence (AI) takes over its creator.
6. Nuclear winter (including EMP blasts) renders the earth uninhabitable.

In classic secular apocalyptic movies, a lone ranger or group of unsuspecting heroes save the planet and humanity by averting disaster despite slim odds. These nail-biting movies are fun due to the happy ending. However, in the last decade or so, many apocalyptic movies end in total despair. There is no hero; people just die. An unhappy ending with no hero protagonist breaks the rules of successful movie scripts – most fail at the box office. Later, I realized many evil people seek a dire ending – humanity destroyed by a government orchestrated event. The bad guys probably sponsored these movies and host premieres in their home.

Modern science fiction movies rarely end well. Human slavery is a recurring theme in many science-fiction movies depicting the future. In many sci-fi flicks, a super-elite class keeps a few slaves to serve them. Inevitably, slaves escape and attempt to bring down the evil dictators only to install a new power-hungry overlord. Others depict a future where humanity is tied into a supercomputer and becomes a slave to machines. The popular *Matrix* movie series shows a ragtag group of freedom fighters fighting against AI machines intent on destroying humanity.[3] The punchline of these movies: we might let you live but as a slave or a serf.

Why are there so many movies about the end of the world? Readers of the Bible understand that the book of Revelation outlines the sequence of events at the end of the world. The Old Testament of the Bible discusses the timetables of the ages in multiple books, including the book of Daniel. Many ancient civilizations depicted the end using petroglyphs etched in the walls of caves. The Mayans predicted the end of the world with their Tzolk'in calendar. Humans remain fascinated with the end of the world, how it happens, and which generation lives in the last chapter. Jesus' disciples asked Him, "Tell us…of the end of the world" (Matt. 24:3 NLT).

Jesus' disciples inquired about the end in part based on the political climate. The heavy-handed Romans demanded the obedience of observant Jews at the time. Overtaxed and oppressed, the Jews did not consider themselves free people. Today, much of humanity feels oppressed. Times are tough, and circumstances don't seem to be improving, causing many to wonder if the present generation will end well. Based on the current turmoil in the world, very few people I speak with today believe things will get better in the near term. Modern preppers plot escape routes when, not if, things get really bad. When consuming movies about the end, I

---

[3] *The Matrix*, dir. The Wachowskis, prod. Joel Silver, 1999.

refused to allow the plots to depress me. With a rewarding career and a wonderful family, my attitude has been, "If it's my time, then *bon voyage!*" As a Christian, I felt comfortable with my place in heaven should I meet my Creator, so I did not sweat it. A few years ago, I gained additional knowledge about the inner workings of the world, and my outlook changed.

Journey Down the Rabbit Hole

A friend and former Wall Street executive began to educate me on the sheer magnitude and breadth of corruption existing in our world today. He explained how the institutions that society depends on do not deserve our trust. He pointed out regularly rigged elections around the world, organized by the true power base: extremely wealthy controllers. Rarely taking the spotlight, they tightly control the world despite appearances to the contrary. These wealthy controllers start and finance wars, regularly manipulating the people through the media and orchestrating brainwashing. At first, I doubted what I heard. I immediately responded, "Why aren't these people mentioned in the *Forbes* wealthiest families list?" Detailed research revealed my friend spoke the truth, and I gained a better understanding of how the world operates.

Over the next couple of years, I became convinced the remarkable power structure ruling the world could not be broken. I thought I needed to devise a plan to get out of dodge if corrupt governments moved against the people. I began to be concerned for my family and researched obscure places on the earth that might be good hiding spots. The sheer brilliance of the global control mechanisms meticulously put in place over centuries impressed me to the point of awe. Over the years, I regularly funded a handful of political organizations and strategic ministries focused on fixing our culture. Our strategic plans typically looked forward a mere year or two. The other side planned in terms of decades – completely outmatching us strategically and financially. From a purely natural perspective I knew the groups I supported fought an unwinnable war.

End Times teaching from my childhood conditioned me to believe things continue to get darker and more dire before Jesus rescued His people in a rapture into the heavens. We all hoped living on earth would not get too bloody before the Rapture came to the rescue! I started to wonder if Hollywood got it right with the tough endings in recent movies about the end. I burned valuable time tracking storm patterns, droughts, wars, and pandemics. Were Christians in for a severe ending? Were we already in the Great Tribulation? I feared for the safety of my loved ones for the first time in my life.

My Dark Days as a Prepper

Preparing for a brutal time on earth set me back in terms of productivity. While I understood how the world *really* worked for the first time in my life, my obsession with End Times and current events alienated friends and family. I dug deep into rabbit holes, some helpful and some not, consuming valuable time and energy and taking me away from my career and life. I began constructing escape routes and preparing bug-out bags. I modified my truck to survive nearly a month in the wilderness and stocked up on expensive long-life camping food. I regularly took my kids on camping trips, trying out new gear just in case I needed to use it to survive the future. Many members of my family thought I lost my mind, and this led to arguments with close loved ones. My fear of the future became debilitating, although I rationalized it as a hobby. However, this hobby began to negatively affect my marriage, business, and personal life. My hobby became an unhealthy obsession that robbed me of important years in hindsight.

In a quest for truth and answers, I scoured books on End Times and studied various theories on how the world would end. My initial instinct – to trust the experts – left me more confused than ever. The *Left Behind* crowd believes we all get rescued in a supernatural event before the earth endures tremendous stress and judgment. Some believe Christians will endure extreme judgment and persecution but are finally relieved (although many die) when Jesus comes to rule the earth. The contradictory theories, while interesting, did not sit right in my heart. I felt somehow Christians failed to recognize the complete picture. How was it possible for me to own a Bible and not know what it says about the future? In ancient times God warned Israel through the prophets of coming dark times and typically gave them the start date, the end date, and the method of deliverance. Did God change? Humanity faces the most impressive control apparatus in history – the modern deep state – operating in lockstep to implement a New World Order, and God did not warn us or let us know how and when it ends? I knew the Bible must have the answers to my questions. In reality, I never searched the Scriptures on the End Times for myself without the help of commentary.

I finally decided to stop consuming analysis from various online channels and books and instead seek truths from the Bible and through prayer. God mercifully gave me new insight from His Word. Hope and expectation took the place of fear and panic. I discovered we live in the most radical and incredible time to be alive since Jesus walked the earth. I am calling it a new name – we live in the time immediately preceding a glorious new age, the Kingdom Age of the Saints.

2. The Church Paralyzed

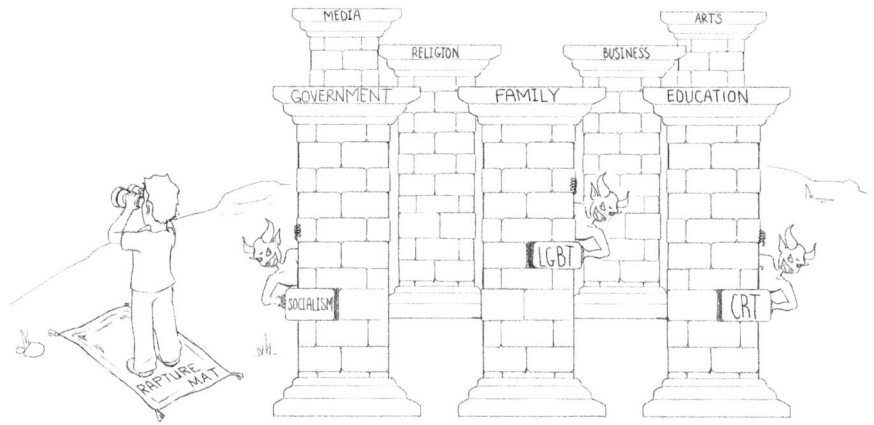

People say that you are alive, but really you are dead. Wake up! Strengthen what you have left before it dies completely. I have found that what you are doing is less than what my God wants.
– Rev 3:1-2 NCV

The book, *The Late Great Planet Earth* by Hal Lindsey was released in the early 1970s and sold nearly 30 million copies. Through it, Christians and non-Christians alike became fascinated with Bible prophecy. The New York Times declared Lindsey's book the Bestselling Nonfiction Book of the 1970s. The book suggested that the anti-Christ, a figure outlined in the Book of Revelation, may already be living. Lindsey's book also highlighted the significance of the creation of the nation of Israel in 1948 and suggested that the "rapture and tribulation" period came next, based upon Bible prophecy. During the tribulation period, those left behind after the Rapture would experience severe conditions under a brutal satanic dictator. The book brought together many specific Biblical scriptures and suggested the world may end within a generation or forty years after the foundation of modern-day Israel.

Thousands of Books on End Times

Many authors made similar predictions in the 1980s and 1990s and more recently. However, nothing happened. Some thought the end of the world would occur because of a massive technical shutdown during Y2K. Designers of early computer systems failed to account for the use of four digits instead of two for a year (e.g., 99 vs. 1999). People expected a massive shutdown of all critical computing systems to occur at the turn of the millennium. At the time I worked at a computer consulting firm making a fortune frantically upgrading client's computer systems to be "Y2K compliant". On New Year's Eve 1999, a diplomatic trip took me to the Middle East, where campfire discussions centered on the end of the world. However, the world did not end on December 31, 1999.

Authors continue to churn out hundreds of books predicting the end of the age based on new Scriptural combinations. I recently heard a message in which a minister humorously observed that many Christians claim, "While the Bible warns we won't know the day and hour, it doesn't mean we won't know the month and the year!" There appears to be a certain "pride" among Biblical scholars concerning their ability to divine predictions within Scripture better than the next person, producing a repeatable cycle of authors writing books with definitive predictions. They gather a following, sell a few books, and then the date passes. Oops! End Times books written to date share a common flaw; writers adopt a fundamental assumption set in stone by modern End Times thinking. They erroneously assume the Rapture occurs as a rescue event in a difficult time.

This theology paralyzed the Church for the last fifty years. Rapture theology became a convenient escape hatch that caused Christians to daydream about heaven, especially during any perceived trial. The very idea of a rapture invigorates our basic fight-or-flight response. Unfortunately, the Rapture means flight for most Christians.

The Prepper Society

Several of my family members tried to predict the exact time of the flight. My dad believed Christians needed to prepare for judgment in America, modern-day Babylon. The strength of his belief caused him to collect and store food in preparation for a food supply shutoff. He hid his food in several obscure places. During prepping breaks, he authored a book to share his insight into America's pending judgment. The food he stored spoiled, and I learned bugs can come out of nowhere and consume things in sealed containers! I remember as a young boy asking Dad, "How can America be judged, given we are the biggest giver to missions in the world?" I still believe God is not finished with America. Many reasons kept me from fully believing my dad's revelation. I hoped to never fall into the same trap of fear leading to stockpiling food and hiding.

During childhood travels with Dad, I realized Christian preppers lived everywhere across the United States. Preppers implemented self-sufficient farming, raised chickens, reloaded their ammunition, and generally distrusted our government. These prepping communities lived off the land and focused on achieving self-sufficiency. They looked for innovative farming ideas and recycled everything. Before green became fashionable, preppers and farmers mastered green living! Preppers avoided big cities. Based on my limited observation, preppers exhibited modest professional growth. I planned to accomplish much in my career and brushed off the prepper group as a fringe.

Most preppers I met spent more time prepping than helping others. Their chief concern focused on protecting their families from the coming tribulation. This form of self-preservation misaligned with my understanding of Jesus' earthly ministry. He laughed off intimidation tactics by both the Jews and Romans during His time on earth. When challenged to pay His taxes, He casually told Peter to catch a fish to find a gold coin within it "lest we should offend them [the tax collectors]" (Matt. 17:27 KJV). The political rulers of the day could not push Jesus around. His ministry and work superseded any political authority of the day. He established the model for us: live boldly, occupy, stay in faith, and when the Lord comes back, He will find productive servants.

The Rapture Removed the Church… From the Fight

Many in the Church subconsciously believe things get worse and worse, then the Lord comes and raptures us home. I call this "rescue rapture" theology. Many church people expect more earthquakes, more disasters, and more chaos and then the rescue rapture comes. According to this way of thinking, God's people suffer under satanic rule until the time when Jesus rescues His people and meets His body (His believers) in the sky and takes them to heaven while the people remaining on the earth undergo extreme turmoil and judgment under the rule of the anti-Christ. There is a scriptural basis for a rapture in the Bible, but the assumptions many Christians make concerning it keep them from reaching their potential. The idea of the Rapture became a fatalistic fantasy escape hatch for these Christians.

If we believe things are going to get worse and worse before our rescue, we will not attempt to improve life on earth. With few exceptions, Christians ignore the geopolitical realm impacting our communities. For instance, Christians largely shunned running for Congress or city council and using their voice on school boards. As a result, we lost tremendous ground to organized secular humanists who have effectively used their voices to change our communities. Then we seem shocked when destructive critical race theory shows up in our public schools, the LGBTQ agenda invades our society, and the freedom to live demonstrating and speaking about our values is taken away. Christians appear to be on the sidelines, doing their best to not offend others who do not yet share their morals or beliefs. The idea of the Rapture rescue created lethargy that became a liability for Christian communities at large.

Imagine you find yourself gripping the roof of your house while waiting for help as torrential flood waters carry you away. Would you take the time to repair a broken roof shingle? Obviously, no. You would hang on for dear life, not bothering to fix anything, believing the house ultimately will be destroyed. Much of the Church takes this posture today. We believe the world blows up during the tribulation, so we don't bother fixing it. Armed with rapture mats in our closets, we keep our heads down hoping to avoid physical detainment by the bad people before the Lord comes. As long as the current governmental authority does not threaten to lock us up, we generally avoid public outcry despite observing significant problems throughout society today. I call this "rapture paralysis."

People believe things will continue to decline no matter what they do, so they don't even try. We sing songs like "I'll Fly Away" and stay within discrete denominational church circles. We shy away from politics, school boards, and polling places because we, in the back of our minds, don't believe it will make a difference. We are consummate watch checkers who work half-hardheartedly, occasionally checking the time. Watch checkers focus on getting out of work rather than throwing themselves into their work. Our rapture watch causes us to miss out on incredible blessings and leadership opportunities in the present time.

I saw a bumper sticker that said, "When I am taken up in the Rapture, you can have my car." Satan loves this mentality. A lender probably possesses title of that person's car, and while the driver idly passes time waiting for the Rapture, Satan schemes and dominates society. Rapture fantasy keeps modern Christians out of the army of effective soldiers for Christ. Instead of living victoriously, taking authority over the devil, and fighting for a free society, we believe the Lord is going to rescue us, so we don't even try to initiate change on earth. When more Christians realize what the Bible says about the future, I hope they will engage society and work to build a better world.

The majority of the world seems to have embraced rapture theology. When big name movie stars are choosing to be in movies about the Rapture, that should signal a problem. Rapture paralysis makes the Church ineffective; We don't use our voice – we appear to have already thrown in the towel. Well known denominations and institutions alike seem to have been subdued without a fight. Why? Because we believe it's inevitable – like when Agent Smith (The Matrix) is talking to Neo (Mr. Anderson), trying to convince him that the future belongs to the Matrix. Remember the line: "You hear that, Mr. Anderson? That is the sound of inevitability. It is the sound of your death. Goodbye, Mr. Anderson."? Agent Smith's point to Neo was that the future was inevitable, set in stone so to speak. This would seem to parallel today's rapture theology. In the movie, however, Neo (Mr. Anderson) decides to fight. As Christians we need to learn how to fight effectively.

You may wonder if I believe there is a rapture of the Church. Yes, but I believe that the Rapture does not occur for probably hundreds of years, during a time when God's people rule the world. The only people on our planet who should legitimately fear the "End Times" are rulers who follow after darkness.

Who Is Our Enemy?

In *The Matrix*, the main character realizes nothing he sees with his physical eyes is real – all is a simulation run by computers. Obviously, *The Matrix* is a science fiction movie. However, in some respects, our reality today is much like the movie. Over thousands of years, our true enemy, Satan, managed to slowly infiltrate a vast majority of institutions and today we find a high degree of godless collaboration among governments and corporations around the world. To fight, we must learn our enemy and his devices. Satan is ruthless, and he hates us. His system offers nothing redeeming for mankind. Satan's current secular world governance system, the fourth beast, represents the most evil system of world government to exist since the time of Noah and the Nephilim rule. It's shockingly treacherous, and more and more people are waking up to the shackles of slavery it creates. But what can we do about it?

Ordinary Heroes – Soldier Saints

In my walk of faith, I learned a very simple truth. I am not waiting on God. He's waiting on me. He recognizes and honors faith on the earth. Second Chronicles 16:9 (AMPC) says that "the eyes of the Lord run to and fro throughout the whole earth to show Himself strong in behalf of those whose hearts are blameless toward Him." The Lord is looking for powerful believers – fearless ones who stretch their faith to move mountains, refusing to lose hope. We are not to bury our talents but use them. We are not to hide our gifts; we are to use them to impact humanity. We are not intimidated by Satan or his system. We are called to be overcomers – modern-day "Soldier Saints."

Today, society longs for real-world heroes. Did you know every hero started as an ordinary person who recognized a need and then tackled it? A hero's journey lacks pleasure during the toil of becoming a hero. There are challenges, setbacks, and often physical danger. Often we don't recognize heroes until later when we hear their story. In the hit movie *Sound of Freedom* we learn the real life story of Tim Ballard, a Special Agent for the Department of Homeland Security who went above and beyond to combat child trafficking rings in Columbia.[4] The film's star, Jim Caviezel, explained in an interview that he wants to inspire moviegoers to *do something* about human trafficking. Sean Feucht *did something* about unconstitutional COVID-19 lockdowns by assembling a small worship band in the middle of the Golden Gate Bridge, defying the mandates. His obedience sparked a revival in many cities around the world. Sean shares how his obedience brought intense persecution, including from the Church. Members of Antifa repeatedly threatened bodily harm to Sean and his family. However, God raised up angel

---

4   *Sound of Freedom*, dir. Alejandro Monteverde, prod. Eduardo Verastegui, 2023.

bodyguards and helped safeguard the movement. Thousands joined the Let Us Worship movement after Sean took the initial step of faith. You see, people are attracted to courage. The ministry of Pastor Rodney Howard-Browne exploded after he was arrested for defying COVID-19 lockdown orders in Florida. He told me, "I wish I got arrested twenty years ago…our ministry took off after my arrest." Tim, Sean, and Rodney heard no audible voice from God telling them to stand up. They simply observed a wrong and decided to do something about it.

In the Bible, we meet Soldier Saint heroes such as Moses, Gideon, and Nehemiah, etc. The backstories of each of these Biblical heroes help us understand that each saw themselves as ordinary people when God called them. Moses stuttered. Gideon, a Biblical prepper, fearfully hid from the brutal government rulers of his day when God approached him to lead. Nehemiah, who rebuilt Jerusalem, started his career as a sommelier (a wine taster). You may be a stay-at-home mother, a schoolteacher, a mechanic, or a high school dropout, however, God can use you to change the world. He is looking for Soldier Saints who exhibit courage in the face of evil. He will provide the right words for you to say, the people to meet, and the resources you need for the mission. Now represents a once-in-a-millennia opportunity to rebuild our world, but it starts with a decision by you to get ready and be bold. Now is the time to seek God for your particular role in the coming kingdom age.

Don't expect the established Church to embrace your mission. The institutionalized Church remains married to rapture theology to the point where most don't fight or provide encouragement to fighters. They seem to have become largely impotent to addressing today's tyranny. A Soldier Saint's journey often starts in a lonely place in the beginning. However, a single act of courage soon attracts a small army to join in the fight. Soon people will recognize you by name.

3. Intelligence Briefing on Our Enemy

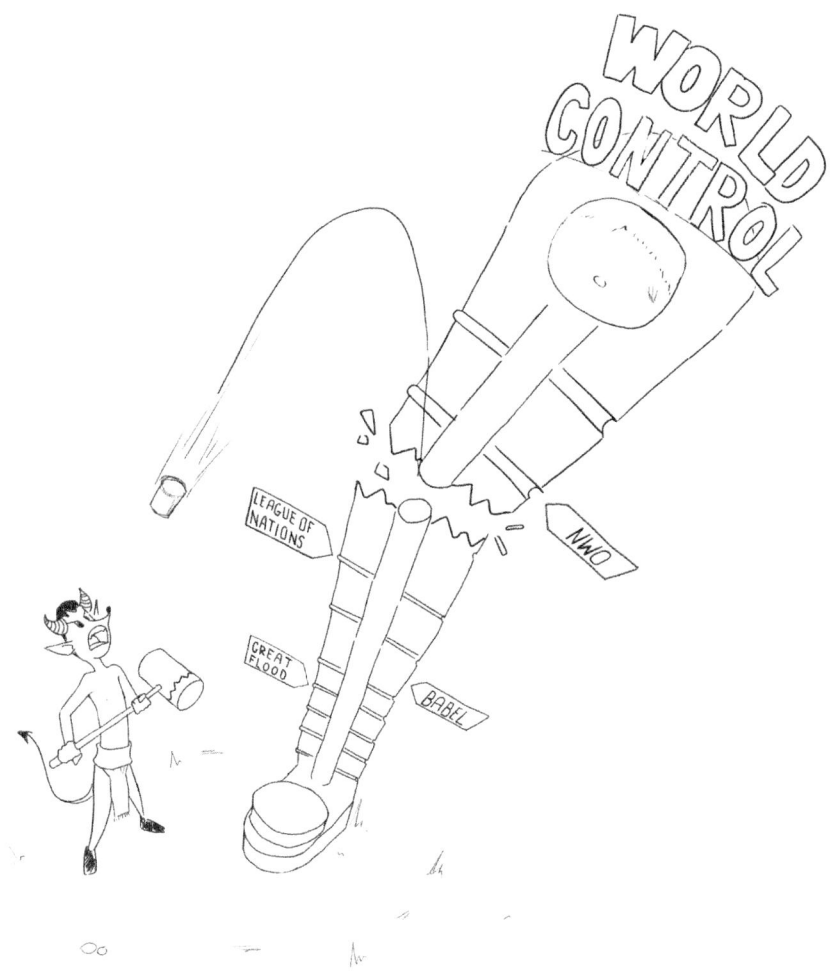

Jesus said, "I saw Satan fall like lightning from heaven."
– Luke 10:18 NCV

Let's begin our training as Soldier Saints with an intelligence briefing on our real enemy. It's impossible to truly understand how the world operates without understanding the methods and history of the enemy of both God and man, Satan. Known for lies and deception, Satan's hatred of God and humanity runs deep. His tools of deception, although limited in number, have succeeded in each generation by tricking certain men and women into going along with his schemes. He only operates because humans were given free will by our Creator, and we each must choose our allegiance. On the other hand, God loves us and if we will let Him, He shows us His glory. Let's walk together through history to understand the various battles Satan has fought with God, and how Satan managed to influence two mighty empires to create the fourth beast system we endure today, merging iron (government) with clay (religion).

The sharper Soldier Saints become at recognizing the roots of tyranny, the more ability they possess as leaders. Tyranny begins with infiltration – a seemingly benign Human Resources Manager or a "woke" salesman intent on destroying your culture. Satan even infiltrated Jesus' disciple group with Judas. However, I believe Jesus knew Judas played a role in God's eternal plan the first day He met him. In general, I find that most Christians lack the acuity and discernment to spot an infiltrator. My experience starting businesses in New York City helped me in this regard. New Yorkers, possessing a large degree of suspicion, typically spotted con artists before others. However, divine discernment and an initial heart check when meeting new people provides the greatest guide in recognizing the intents of others. Satan, the master con artist, possesses an expert skill in infiltrating organizations. Let's take a look at his methods so we can avoid letting him wreck our dreams.

Satan's Banishment from Heaven

Before he appeared in the Garden of Eden, Satan hatched a scheme, a murderous campaign, to destroy mankind (John 10:10 and John

8:44). When God created humans in His image, Satan, a fallen angel, burned with jealousy. Satan may even have been the unnamed angel questioning God's judgment in creating mankind in Psalm 8. In the psalm, the beautiful revelation of God's plan for humanity to be crowned with glory and honor is called into question. Other scripture describes how Satan attempted to exalt himself above God (Isa. 14:14), causing him to fall like lightning, damaging the earth during his forceful ejection from heaven (Luke 10:18, Gen. 1:2). Scripture indicates Satan convinced a third of the angelic hosts to join in the fight against God, ultimately falling from grace along with Satan (Rev 12:4). Satan and his army of traitorous angels fell to a reduced and miserable state after his attempt to ascend to heaven and take over the throne of God failed. Over the course of thousands of years, Satan has influenced humans to join him in his fight against God.

Fall of Man in the Garden of Eden

To this day, Satan attempts to control and destroy humankind using all forms of conniving and trickery to achieve his goal. As a first move after his fall, Satan subdued the serpent and used its cunning to fulfill his purpose: to tempt Adam. It says in Genesis 3:1 that the serpent was more subtle (crafty, shrewd, sensible) than any beast of the field that God had made. Satan coerced the creature to perform his dirty work. Why would the serpent willingly lend his body to Satan so he could gain entrance into the Garden? It is possible Satan promised the serpent that its seed would one day rule the earth as his leader, the anti-Christ. Satan's offer appealed to the serpent, and he took the deal. Through the serpent, Satan told Eve that she and Adam would be like God if they ate the forbidden fruit. After the serpent yielded his body and Adam and Eve lost their authority in the Garden of Eden, God judged the serpent in Genesis 3:15 (AMPC), stating: "I will put enmity between you and the woman, and between your offspring and her Offspring; he will bruise and tread your head underfoot, and you will lie in wait and bruise His heel." Here we get a picture of the serpent's seed or bloodline ruling as the anti-Christ himself. If we read the Bible, it does not end well for the serpent's seed, for his head gets crushed in three distinct ways. The first occurs during the triumph of the cross (Col. 2:15). The second crushing occurs when God judges the leaders of the fourth beast, avenging the blood of martyrs and ending a long-standing reign of tyranny (Rev 6:15). The third crushing occurs when Jesus defeats Satan's supreme leader, the anti-Christ (Rev 19:20). Satan is a liar and won't be able to make good on his promises to the serpent's bloodline because God's Word always prevails. The effects of the serpent's bloodline can be seen even today in spiritually depraved people who readily accept all forms of demonic influence.

Stripped of his original glory after yielding to Satan in the Garden of Eden, Adam died spiritually, bringing a curse on his progeny. I imagine God in this moment extremely sad and grieved at heart even though He knew His children would fall. God also already had a plan to restore humanity. None of these events caught God by surprise. However, Satan used his initial foothold to progressively tempt humans to organize governments under his rule with one common theme and end goal: to rob God of His prized creation and pervert the order of creation. Satan recognized the creative power only found in humans who are the only members of creation that were specifically created in God's image and likeness. Satan needs to influence humans in order to fulfill his purpose and he continues to use the same temptation that worked on Adam, that he could be equal with God, with all following generations. Satan's sole intent is to organize and influence mankind to the point of self-destruction, thus thwarting God's will.

The Days of Noah and the Flood

By the days of Noah, the world had morally declined to the point where Satan nearly achieved his goal of world control. Evil and debauchery prevailed, and giants (the Nephilim) ruled the world. Some Bible scholars believe the Nephilim were the offspring of fallen angels or "sons of God" and the daughters of men. This mysterious time produced a low point for humanity – the entire civilization was evil, and only one family still heard and listened to God's voice and lived righteously. The world population received judgment as a result. The flood wiped out all creation except for Noah's and his sons' families (and possibly their servants). After this, God promised He would never judge the world again with a flood and provided a rainbow in the sky as a sign of His promise. It could appear that the LGBTQ community adopted the rainbow as their flag to taunt God by using His chosen symbol of mercy.

First World Government – Nimrod and Babel

After the great flood, Satan regrouped. He influenced Nimrod, a mighty man and descendant of Cain who was an enemy of Abraham and a tyrannical ruler. Some theorize Nimrod likely came from the Nephilim bloodline because the Bible refers to him as a "mighty man". (It is theorized the Nephilim bloodline survived the flood by being reactivated after the great flood through Ham, the rebellious son of Noah.)[5] Inspired by Satan, Nimrod hatched a plan to organize

---

5   Laura Sanger, *The Roots of the Federal Reserve* (Dallas: Relentlessly Creative Books, 2020), 120.

in Babel (modern-day Iraq) and the leaders of that time acted with one mind and of one accord, building a tower to ascend unto the throne of God and again be like (or equal to) God. (The tower also served as a manmade protection from another flood.) Some speculate the tower was a Stargate to unlock a portal – an Einstein-Rosen Bridge that would lead to the heavenly throne, which would be the fulfillment of a satanic dream.[6] Nimrod represents the first world leader in recorded history. He fueled humanism among the citizens of Babel by setting a goal of achieving interaction with gods. In Babylonia, the gods did not descend in order to walk with humans but rather to lie with them. The practice involved sexual rituals inside the ziggurat temple.[7] Satan once again demonically influenced humans to attempt to achieve his goal. In response God confused their language and easily thwarted this plan. Today with online digital translation, humans have devised a way to overcome this language barrier.

Ancient Egypt

Ancient Egypt prospered mightily with the benefit of a large slave labor force, namely Israelites, who through their ancestor Abraham had established a covenant relationship with God. Ancient Egypt practiced pagan worship of graven images, such as the four-winged divine serpent Chnuphis and deified their rulers as gods. God supernaturally delivered Israel from their captives as recorded in the Old Testament of the Bible (see details in Chapter 8).

---

6 Thomas Horn and Cris Putnam, *On the Path of the Immortals: Exo-Vaticana Project L.U.C.I.F.E.R. and the Strategic Locations Where Entities Await the Appointed Time* (Crane, MO: Defender, 2015), 175.

7 A. Annus, "On the Origin of the Watchers: A Comparison Study of the Antediluvian Wisdom of Mesopotamia and Jewish Traditions," *Journal for the Study of Pseudepigrapha* 19, no. 5 (1991): 277-320.

Kingdom of Israel and Judah

After God delivered Israel from Egyptian slavery and transferred Egypt's wealth to them, following a forty-year hiatus in the desert, Israel conquered many lands and formed a great kingdom led by a succession of kings, including King David. King David's son, Solomon, built an exquisite temple that housed the glory of God as well as the ark of the covenant, a golden box containing important items demonstrating the covenant God made with Israel as His chosen people. More importantly, the glory and fire of God dwelt among the Israelites bound by this strong covenant. As long as Israel followed God's commands, they prospered. God specifically commanded Israel to annihilate all remaining giants (the Nephilim), a genetic defilement of God's creation. He also commanded them to not intermarry with foreigners, and to avoid worshiping pagan idols. Israel only partially obeyed God's commandments and ultimately suffered defeat by the Babylonians. God provided multiple warnings to Israel before their destruction and let them know their exile under the Babylonians would last seventy years (Jer. 25:11).

The end of the kingdom of Israel ushered in the times of the Gentiles, which Jesus referred to in Luke 21:24. Merriam Webster's dictionary defines Gentile as "pagan." Israel no longer exercised geopolitical rule during this time, rather four successive secular empires would rule the world, beginning with Babylon. I believe that the times of the Gentiles corresponds to the opening of the seals in Revelation 6. The first four seals represent the first four secular kingdoms or beast governments, described as the "four horsemen" in Revelation 6.

Figure 1 shows the sequence of the various secular empires described in the book of Daniel up to the time of the stone judgment.

For a more detailed depiction showing the timeline and additional detail, visit revelationriddle.com.

Figure 1: Biblical Sequence Leading up to the Stone Judgment

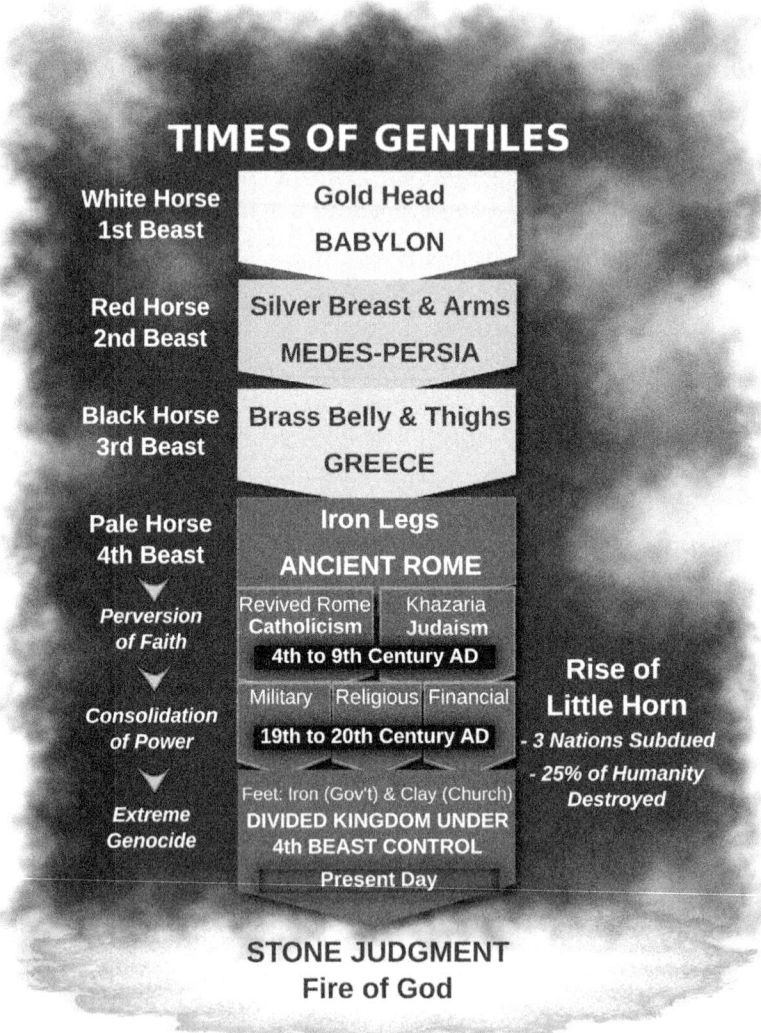

The Times of the Gentiles

Babylon (605 BC to 539 BC)[8]: The White Horse

"I saw a white horse. Its rider carried a bow and was given a victory garland. He rode off victorious, conquering right and left."

– Rev 6:1-2 MSG

After the Babylonians defeated Israel in battle, they destroyed Solomon's temple and carried off the temple gold. Many Israelites were killed and scattered, although a remnant survived. Now exiled and serving as an aid to the Babylonian King Nebuchadnezzar, the prophet Daniel began to interpret and receive dreams and visions, which he wrote down (the book of Daniel). God outlined a timetable and series of events for the four consecutive secular empires. Daniel also wrote about what would happen after the four secular empires ran their course, leading into the stone judgment, when God judges the four beasts. Daniel also prophesied what happens after the stone judgment. (We'll get to that in later chapters.)

Babylon, the first beast system, represents a revived Babel from the days of Nimrod, with similar types of pagan worship and practices. The Babylonians routinely mocked God and were known to sacrifice humans to Marduk and Baal, their gods. Sexual immorality pervaded the culture. The Babylonians built an impenetrable capital city on the same plain where Babel was built. Always several steps ahead, God devised a plan to topple Babylon before its formation. His prophets spoke of a leader who would defeat Babylon some two

---

[8] D. J. Wiseman, "Babylonia 605–539 B.C.," in *Cambridge Ancient History,* ed. John Boardman, I. E. S. Edwards, E. Sollberger, and N. G. L. Hammond, 2nd ed., Cambridge: Cambridge University Press, 1992), 3:229–51.

hundred years before the Persian King Cyrus's birth. (A detailed account of the defeat of Babylon is contained in Chapter 8.)

Medo-Persia (539 BC to 331 BC)[9]: The Red Horse

"Another horse appeared, this one red. Its rider was off to take peace from the earth, setting people at each other's throats, killing one another. He was given a huge sword."

– Rev 6:4

Isaiah, Jeremiah, and Daniel all prophesied that the Medes and Persians would topple the Babylonian Empire. The first Persian Empire became one of the largest empires in history, stretching from Europe's Balkan Peninsula in the West to India's Indus Valley in the East.[10] The massive conquests under the Persians fulfilled Revelation 6:4, which states the red horse was given the ability to take peace from the earth with a great sword. Daniel remained prominent in the Medo-Persia Empire and served as a trusted adviser to King Darius. Medo-Persia worshiped images of Baal and a dragon. A key event during the Medo-Persia Empire, chronicled in the book of Esther, involved a satanic attempt to wipe out the entire bloodline of God's chosen people. Haman, a senior adviser to King Artaxerxes, hatched a genocidal plan to destroy the people of Israel by inducing the king to pass a law to kill anyone who would not worship the king, thus dooming the Israelites who worshiped God. The plan backfired on Haman, and the king executed Haman instead. The story offers interesting insight into how Satan works;

---

9   "Achaemenid Empire", accessed June 13, 2023, *Wikipedia.org*, https://en.wikipedia.org/wiki/Achaemenid_Empire
10 "Persian Empire," *History*, updated May 30, 2023, https://www.history.com/topics/ancient-middle-east/persian-empire.

When he possesses geopolitical power through a willing leader, Satan seeks to destroy God's people and wipe out their bloodline.

Under Medo-Persia, God's temple in Jerusalem was rebuilt and the Israelites once again worshiped God according to the covenant of Moses. The rebuilding of the temple despite secular rule foreshadows future years when Christianity thrived without Christian leaders exercising dominion in geopolitical form.

Greece (331 BC to c. 146 BC): The Black Horse

"A black horse this time. Its rider carried a set of scales in his hand. I heard a message...'A quart of wheat for a day's wages, or three quarts of barley, but the oil and wine you want.'"

– Rev 6:5-6

The Greek kingdom, described in advance of its existence in Daniel chapters 2, 8, and 11, defeated Medo-Persia and ended up controlling Jerusalem. In 167 BC, Antiochus set up an altar to the Greek god Zeus inside the Judean temple and sacrificed a pig on it. Antiochus subsequently required pagan sacrifices in all the Judean villages, sparking the Maccabean Revolt. Israel then regained their freedom for a time and later the Roman Senate recognized Israel as an independent state. The Greeks worshiped many different gods and ritualistic human sacrifice to multiple gods remained common in Greek religion. It was believed to be necessary to appease the gods. The Greeks also instituted mathematics, philosophy, science, and democracy. In Revelation 6:5-6, John describes the man who sat on the black horse as one with a pair of balances in his hand, signifying the order that the Greece society introduced to humanity.

Ancient Rome (c. 146 BC to AD 476): The Pale Horse

"A colorless horse, sickly pale. Its rider was Death, and Hell was close on its heels. They were given power to destroy a fourth of the earth by war, famine, disease, and wild beasts".

– Rev 6:8

The books of Revelation and Daniel directly mention the fourth beast while indirect references to the fourth beast are found in many other books of the Bible. Most Scholars agree that the fourth beast is rooted in the Roman Empire, which historians believe was consolidated under Caesar Augustus in 27 BC. Some historians point out that Rome consolidated power earlier – Rome had achieved mini-empire status as early as 201 BC after their victory in the Second Punic War. Rome destroyed Corinth, the last remaining Greek stronghold, in 146 BC.[11] Rome sacked Athens, now ruled by the kingdom of Pontus (an attempted resurrection of the Persian Empire, which was joined in the fight against Rome by some Greeks) in 86 BC and finally destroyed the remainder of the kingdom of Pontus in 63 BC.[12]

Rome began conquests of Mediterranean seaside villages, hence the description of the beast coming out of the sea in the book of Daniel (Dan. 7:3) and Revelation (Rev 13:1). Unlike the prior three beast systems (Babylon, Medo-Persia, and Greece) that functioned primarily as monarchies, the fourth beast featured ten horns representing ten kingdoms. In other words, the fourth beast exercised dominion not through a singular ruler but through a league

---

[11] Franco Cavazzi, "The Early Roman Republic", *Roman-Empire.net*, accessed June 6, 2023, https://roman-empire.net/republic/early-republic.
[12] "Kingdom of Pontus", *Wikipedia.org*, accessed June 13, 2023, https://en.wikipedia.org/wiki/Kingdom_of_Pontus.

of nations or kingdoms. The league of nations within the fourth beast system works together to accomplish more than the prior three beast systems. The vision of the fourth beast terrified the prophet Daniel and gave him nightmares.

The Romans, an Aryan race, who Jewish scholars believe are descendants of Esau or Edomites, invaded and conquered the Italian peninsula from the north.[13] Rome began as a pagan empire, distinctly known for worship of the sky god (Jupiter) and the war god (Mars or Ceres) who both represented gods of the state. As Rome conquered other lands, they incorporated additional gods, such as Diana, into their religion. They constructed large elaborate temples in honor of their gods, including on the Capitoline Hill in Rome, a shrine to Jupiter, and the Temple of Vesta, a circular building where human offerings were sacrificed to gods. Throughout Roman history the priest functioned not as the mediator between the gods and man but for the purpose of state worship. To Rome, the regulation of human dealings, the body of civil law, and acts of worship all fell under the category of legal contracts.[14] Numerous priestly orders, known as the Sacred College, managed hundreds of government bureaus, meeting along with the senators in the temples to conduct state business.[15]

During the Roman occupation of Jerusalem prior to its destruction in AD 70, Rome appointed pro-Roman rulers of Judea, who would handpick the Jewish high priests.[16] One appointed ruler, Herod the Great, the son of Idumean Antipater, a convert to Judaism,

---

[13] William Beeston, *The Roman Empire of the Edomite* (np: 1858), 4.
[14] Cyril Bayiley, "Roman Religion", *The Encyclopaedia Britannica*, 11th ed. (Cambridge, UK: Cambridge University Press, 1911), 23:577-594.
[15] F. Tupper Saussy, *Rulers of Evil: Useful Knowledge About Governing Bodies* (Santa Monica, CA: Ospray, 2001), 10-11.
[16] Israel Abrahams, "Jews", *The Encyclopaedia Britannica*, 11th ed. (Cambridge, UK: Cambridge University Press, 1911), 15:398.

attempted to destroy Jesus soon after His birth by slaughtering all children under the age of two in Bethlehem.[17] Herod had heard from wise men and prophets that Jesus could replace him as king of the Judeans (Matt. 2). During this period in Judean history, there was a mixture of the Idumeans (Edomites) with the Judeans (descendants of Jacob). Empowered by Rome, the Idumeans used Judaism as a means to achieve their goal of dominion over the usurpers of their inheritance, the Israelites. The strategy was to either cast off Judaism in favor of Hellenism (e.g., Greco-Roman worship) or pervert it into a false Judaism (the tradition of the elders).[18] Later, the Romans attempted to permanently root out Judaism during the Jewish-Roman wars in the first and second century AD, resulting in one and a half to over three million deaths.[19]

Historians commonly state the Roman Empire fell in AD 476, upon the deposition of Emperor Romulus Augustulus.[20] However, the Roman senate continued to meet, and Roman law continued to govern the land. Roman armies continued to fight and win victories on the frontier. In the next chapter, I lay out the case that the Rome-rooted fourth beast continues to operate to the present day, albeit in a different form from ancient Rome.

The Birth of Christianity (4 BC to AD 30)

Jesus Christ, born in Bethlehem in about 4 BC, began His ministry when He was around thirty years of age. No single person has ever changed the course of history to the degree that Jesus Christ did.

---

17 J. Bigland, *A Compendious History of the Jews* (London: 1820), 179.
18 Sanger, *Roots of the Federal Reserve*, 258.
19 "List of wars by death toll," *Wikipedia.org*, accessed June 7, 2023, https://en.wikipedia.org/wiki/List_of_wars_by_death_toll.
20 Alen S, "Fall of the Western Roman Empire 476 AD," *Short History*, September 28, 2016, https://tinyurl.com/22yr9njz.

To many Judeans, Jesus represented the long-promised Messiah, as prophesied by Isaiah and many others. To both the Pharisees and the Romans, Jesus represented a political threat. Crucified by the Romans in roughly AD 30, Jesus rose from the dead, and many followers witnessed the risen Christ. Christ is not Jesus' last name; Christ means "the anointed one," a term to describe the power and presence of God being upon Jesus. Satan endured major defeats during Jesus' ministry and especially at the time of His resurrection. Jesus, wholly innocent yet cursed under the law, rose from the dead and broke the power of the law, freeing humans and offering salvation as well as close communion with God by accepting Jesus as their personal Lord and Savior.

The early Church met in very plain buildings with no special markings. The focus remained on repentance, salvation, miracles, and baptism by both water and the Holy Spirit. Because Rome, especially under the Emperor Nero, persecuted the Christians, church leaders sometimes met in secret and preferred simple meeting places. It was not until Rome adopted Christianity centuries later that churches begin to look more like the temples of Rome.

The Forgotten Empire: Khazaria (c. AD 500 to AD 1000)

Around the time of the fall of ancient Rome, an empire formed that served as an important springboard for a tribe of people who ultimately wielded great power within the fourth beast system. Although the Khazars successfully infiltrated many government and religious institutions very little is taught in modern history about them and many people have never even heard of Khazaria. However, Khazaria produced a fierce band of infiltrators that successfully gained power by introducing chaos more than any other people group of this time.

The Khazarians, a semi-nomadic Turkic-Ugrian people, began expanding their power base to include eastern Ukraine, Crimea, southern Russia, and other countries beginning in seventh century AD.[21] They established the Khazar Kingdom which included most of Eastern Europe. The early Khazars, apparent mercenaries with a thirst for plunder and revenge, were called upon to defend the Persians initially and later, the Romans.[22] At the height of the Khazar empire, they made their fortune on maritime tariffs by controlling the critical trade route between the Far East, the Middle East, and Europe.[23] As a tribe, they practiced shamanism which involved occult ceremonies often featuring human sacrifice, the cult of the sacred forest, and worship of fire, thunder, and lightning.[24] In roughly AD 800, Khazarians "claimed" Judaism as their religion, primarily for convenience and self-preservation under pressure from surrounding nations which were repulsed by their shamanistic practices.[25] The Khazars, especially their ruling class, imported Rabbinic Judaism based upon the Babylonian Talmud.[26] However, they still continued their shamanistic rituals, violating the teachings of the Torah (the first five books of the Old Testament). In approximately AD 1000, the Russian czar led a group of nations to invade Khazaria in an attempt to stop the Khazarian torture and murder of children from countries

---

21 "Khazar," *Britannica.com*, accessed April 21, 2023, www.britannica.com/topic/Khazar.
22 Charles Norton Edgcumbe Eliot, "Khazars", *The Encyclopaedia Britannica*, 11th ed. (Cambridge, UK: Cambridge University Press, 1911), 15:775.
23 "Khazar", *The Encyclopedia of Islam*, new ed. (Leiden, Netherlands: E.J. Brill, 2007), 4:1177.
24 Julian Baldick, *Animal and Shaman: Ancient Religions of Central Asia* (New York: New York University Press, 2000), 30. See also "Khazar", Encyclopedia of Islam, 4:1173.
25 Preston James and Mike Harris, "Hidden History of the Incredibly Evil Khazarian Mafia," *Covert Geopolitics*, March 11, 2015,
 https://geopolitics.co/2015/03/11/hidden-history-of-the-incredibly-evil-khazarian-mafia.
26 Zvi Ankori, *Karaites in Byzantium: The Formative Years, 970-1100*, (New York: AMS Press, 1968), 64-86.

adjacent to Khazaria. After the invasion many Khazarians fled with their vast wealth of silver and gold, migrating into Western Europe.[27]

Satan's Infiltration of Christianity

Satan's favorite technique is to take something pure and good and twist it into evil and idolatry. Christianity began with Jesus and His twelve disciples and then expanded to the seventy (Luke 10 and 11; John 10) and then the 120 in the upper room (Acts 1:15 and Acts 2) and then spread throughout the world. By the fourth century, Christianity had spread throughout the Roman Empire, and Rome itself decided to adopt Christianity as the state religion, however, this constituted a political merger at best. Rome saw itself as the "god of the state" representing the interest of the people to the gods. In essence, Christianity under Rome provided yet another framework to incorporate into their state worship and another method to place additional controls on mankind. The popularity of Christianity actually helped Rome to hold onto their power. To the hardcore cynic, during the times of the Crusades, Christianity provided Rome with a new reason to invade other countries for spoil while at the same time forcing conversion to Rome's version of Christianity.

When Emperor Constantine formally adopted Christianity as the empire's official religion in the fourth century, the considerable wealth of the pagan priests who owned half the lands and one fourth of the population, immediately became the possession of the Christian churches when the Roman priests declared themselves to be Christians.[28] The pagan gods were then renamed to be considered appropriate to Christianity. For example, the Temple

---
27 James and Harris, "Hidden History."
28 Saussy, Rulers of Evil, 10-11.

of Apollo became the Church of St. Apollinaris, and the Temple of Mars became the Church of Santa Martina. Icons of Apollo with a halo were re-identified as Jesus. The sign over the Pantheon which read: "To Cybele [the fertility goddess] and All the Gods" was rewritten as: "To Mary and All the Saints," deifying Mary and the church leaders. Pope Leo I decreed: "St. Peter and St. Paul have replaced Romulus and Remus as Rome's protecting patrons," quite possibly beginning the tradition of praying to saints for protection. Government continued without interruption during the merger of Christianity with Rome. Consequently, through the intermixing of the old pagan symbolism of sun worship and other relics of the past, pagan religious practices crept into Christianity under the banner of Roman Catholicism. Rome, no stranger to religious worship melding with government, now possessed an additional tool and Christianity, now part of the power base of the ancient Roman Empire, became firmly integrated within the state.

In the Book of Ezekiel, the prophet excoriated the religious leaders for worshiping idols in addition to their temple worship of God. God showed Ezekiel in a dream that the religious leaders were secretly worshiping and offering incense to the sun god and other gods. This abominable sin disqualified Israel from receiving God's blessing and ultimately led to their being conquered by the Babylonians. To this day, the worship of other gods remains an egregious affront to God. When the Romans adopted Christianity as their state religion and intermixed Christianity with sun worship or deified men to be worthy of worship, it was as evil to God as it was in the time of Ezekiel. Nimrod, the original leader of Babel, also worshiped the sun and made himself a god along with Semiramis, the moon goddess. As a consequence, God destroyed Babel's progress by confusing the people's language so they could no longer effectively communicate and understand each other. God has never changed; He is not pleased with idolatry.

Satan's Infiltration of Judaism

When Jesus took on the Pharisees during His earthly ministry, He challenged the tradition of the elders which the Pharisees considered to be on par with the law of Moses. Jesus declared of the Pharisees, "Their worship is a farce, for they teach man-made ideas as commands from God" (Matt. 15:9 NLT). Undeterred, the Pharisees continued to develop and refine their oral tradition. The Pharisaic tradition later morphed into modern Judaism (or modern rabbinism), through the adoption of the Babylonian Talmud.[29] The Babylonian Talmud, completed in roughly AD 500, is considered to be the pinnacle of modern Rabbinic Judaism; its authority relating to Jewish law supersedes the Torah in Judaism.[30] Only a tiny sect within Judaism – the Karaites, representing less than one third of one percent of the Jewish population – treat the Torah (the first five books of the Old Testament) as the exclusive commandments to the Jews. However, the orthodox Jewish rabbinate historically despises and severely persecutes the Karaites. The vast majority of modern Jews consider the Babylonian Talmud to be replacement law to the Torah.

So, what does the Babylonian Talmud teach? Generally, the Babylonian Talmud contains three main themes. The first theme is Jewish supremacy; Jews have superior legal status and may legally cheat, rob, and kill non-Jews. The Talmud specifically identifies

---

[29] Louis Finkelstein, *The Pharisees: The Sociological Background of Their Faith*, 3rd ed. (Philadelphia: Jewish Publication Society of America, 1966), 1:xx-xxi.
[30] "Talmud," *Wikipedia.org*, accessed June 5, 2023, https://en.wikipedia.org/wiki/Talmud.

Christians and contains laws allowing adherents to kill Christians and confiscate their property without committing sin.[31] This was common even during the time Jesus walked the earth as those in spiritual power struggled to maintain their status quo. The second theme found within the Babylonian Talmud is hatred toward "Goys" or Gentiles. In the Talmud, claims are made that Gentiles are subhuman animals that prefer sex with cows. The third theme found within the Talmud is extreme blasphemies against Jesus Christ and the Virgin Mary. These blasphemies are too vile to reprint. There are also allowances in the Talmud for Jews to have sex with children with no consequence. Perhaps the Babylonian Talmud is best summed up in a quote by Israeli Sephardic leader Rabbi Ovadia Yosef, when he said, "Goyim were born only to serve us. Without that, they have no place in the world; only to serve the people of Israel."[32]

Critics of the modern form of Judaism today are quickly labeled by the media as anti-Semitic, implying anti-Hebrew. This term strikes fear in most as the commonly accepted narrative considers Jews to be descended from the residents of the kingdom of Judah, who were exiled for thousands of years and eventually returned to their native land, the modern-day state of Israel. However, new studies based on comprehensive genetic data refute this commonly accepted narrative that modern-day Jews descended from the kingdom of Judah. Researcher Eran Elhaik conducted extensive research at the School of Public Health at Johns Hopkins University in Baltimore. He found that among Central European and East European Jews,

---

31 Benjamin H. Freedman, *Facts Are Facts* (Carson City, NV: Bridger House, 1954), 71-72.
32 Syarif Hidayat, "The Satanic Verses of the Jewish Talmud and Zionism," *hshidayat*, accessed June 5, 2023, https://hshidayat.wordpress.com/2014/01/07/the-satanic-verses-of-the-jewish-talmud- and-zoinism.

the Khazar component is expressed as most dominant in their genome, accounting for 38 percent and 30 percent, respectively. Whereas, the genome of the origin of Jews from the kingdom of Judah, where Jesus was born, was statistically insignificant.[33] Why is this important?

God formed a covenant with Abraham. I believe God has special plans for the true descendants of Jacob. Just like God is not done with America, God is not done with Israel. Many ministries feel called to evangelize Jews and there is absolutely nothing wrong with that. We must recognize, however, that the Hebrew Bible (the Torah) is a divinely inspired work that actually points people to Jesus as the Messiah. Whereas the Babylonian Talmud is a newer rabbinical commentary that actually ridicules Jesus and His followers. Generally, most Christians believe that any group of people that author a new bible loosely based on the Hebrew Bible is a cult. For instance, most Christians accuse Mormons of belonging to a cult, because they wrote their own bible (the Book of Mormon) making changes that erode the sovereignty of Christ. A vast majority of modern Jews don't follow the Hebrew Bible, they follow their own bible, the Babylonian Talmud. Jesus called this form of worship by the Jewish scholars of His time a "farce" in Matthew 15:9. Was Jesus being anti-Semitic when He made this statement?

Satanic Hatred for Christians and Judeans

It's important to understand how Satan "rules" the world from a high level in order to be able to recognize his methods at the micro level. Christians today are largely naive concerning the inner

---

33 Ofer Aderet, "The Jewish People's Ultimate Treasure Hunt," *Haaretz*, December 28, 2012, www.haaretz.com/2012-12-28/ty-article/.premium/the-jewish-peoples-ultimate-treasure-hunt/0000017f-f70a-d47e-a37f-ff3e820d0000.

workings of Satan's power structure on earth. Because Satan could not achieve equality with God, he hates humans who are created in God's image. When Satan infiltrates Judaism or Christianity, he then hates the real followers and tries to destroy them. The apparent hatred many Khazarian rabbinic Jews have toward both Christians and genuine Judean ancestors (many of whom accepted Jesus as Messiah) would appear to manifest from satanic motivation. Satan knows in the time of the very end, that time when he rules through a penultimate anti-Christ, the Judean bloodline remnant of the twelve tribes of Israel will still serve as a thorn in his side, disrupting his plans with hard core evangelism via the 144,000 End Times soldiers in Revelation 7:4. The "Judean blood wars," the quest to extinguish the bloodline of the authentic Judeans, is not new – it goes all the way back to Haman, Herod, and, in modern times, Hitler.

The satanic blood wars are prophesied in the Bible. Revelation 12 verses 3-4, 13-14, and 17 (AMPC, with bracketed explanations) describe the spiritual war:

> Behold, a huge, fiery-red dragon, with seven heads and ten horns [the fourth beast of Daniel 7:7] ...stationed himself in front of the woman who was about to be delivered [Mary, the mother of Jesus] so that he might devour her child [Jesus] as soon as she brought it forth [Dan. 8:10] (Rev 12:3-4)

> ...[A]nd he [the dragon] went in pursuit of the woman who had given birth to the male Child [Mary's bloodline]...But the woman was supplied with the two wings of a giant eagle so she might fly ...where she is to be kept safe and fed for a time, and times, and half

a time [Dan. 7:25 and 12:7, see also chapter 4 of this book] (Rev 12:13-14).

...So the dragon was furious (enraged) at the woman, and went away to wage war on the remainder of her descendants - [on those] who obey God's commandments [Judeans]...and who have the testimony of Jesus Christ [and adhere to it and bear witness to Him (Christians)] (Rev 12:17).

Note that the Bible promises that God protects a remnant of the Judean bloodline despite Satan's best efforts! Christians today should learn to interpret the times properly, recognizing the difference between the Judean ancestors, God's elect, and the Khazarian imposters who appear to hate both Christians and Judeans alike.

The dragon mentioned in Revelation 12 seeks to destroy Christians, not just the Judean bloodline. The dragon, a term considered to be synonymous with Satan, influences many forms of organized religion and government to murder Christians in the time of the fourth beast – especially those anointed with God's power. For instance, ancient Rome sacrificed Christians for sport in the Coliseum and ultimately killed all the disciples except the apostle John. Despite professing Christianity, the early Roman Catholic Church aggressively murdered "heretics" who owned Bibles or who questioned the legitimacy of several pagan ideals contained within Catholic teaching, calling them Protestants (from the root word protest). The Islamic state as well has murdered many Christians over the years. Less than one hundred years ago, the Bolshevik communists murdered nearly 70 million Russians, mostly Christian. Christian persecution continues worldwide, reaching unprecedented levels and today it's estimated that 360 million Christians, or one in seven worldwide, are experiencing "high levels" of persecution and discrimination for their faith, with thirteen Christians killed (martyred) daily for their faith.[34] Soon Soldier Saints will put an end to this persecution and lead the world.

---

34 "World Watch List 2023," *Open Doors*, accessed June 6, 2023, www.opendoors.org/en-US/persecution/countries.

4. Butchers in Suits and Gowns

Then he said to me, "This fourth beast is the fourth world power that will rule the earth. It will be different from all the others. It will devour the whole world, trampling and crushing everything in its path.

– Dan. 7:23 NLT

After the fall of ancient Rome, the fourth beast began to consolidate power using a form of Christianity and Judaism – both rife with idolatry and compromise following satanic infiltration. Power brokers, claiming either Christian or Jewish heritage, began to rule from behind-the-scenes, even working together no matter their heritage. Gone are the days of walled cities, inviting attack. A far more effective replacement is a legalized monopoly of like-minded behind-the-scenes conspirators intent upon world control. A great consolidation of power occurred during the nineteenth and twentieth centuries, accompanied by a period of extreme genocide. Based on historical data, the current genocide remains unrivaled by any prior genocide in terms of body count. The banking and finance system serves as the fortress of the fourth beast in modern times, providing the wealth to influence all but the most ardent pursuers of righteousness.

Rome Revived

Rome was revived and reestablished under Emperor Justinian in AD 555.[35] The centuries that followed demonstrated the effectiveness of the extension of religious rule, namely the Roman Catholic Church. During this time, Christian revivals or even owning a Bible constituted heresy to the Roman Catholic Church and resulted in much bloodshed and war. Various monarchies emerged, most with varying degrees of influence under the Roman Church. Along the way several nations attempted to exercise full control of the fourth beast system, such as during the time of the Ottoman Empire. However, no singular visible king rules the fourth beast system, rather a

---

[35] Aleksa Vucčković, "Emperor Justinian the Great: The Life and Rule of a Visionary Roman," updated August 10, 2019, *ancient-origins.net*, www.ancient-origins.net/history-famous-people/emperor-justinian-0012422.

group of nations collectively implements the destructive power of the fourth beast.

The Roman-originated fourth beast lives today. In Revelation 1:1, John explains that his revelation includes events that must "shortly come to pass," signifying the future. Again, in Revelation 4:1 (ASV), Jesus tells John, "Come up hither, and I will show thee the things which must come to pass hereafter." John describes a near mirror description of Daniel's vision of the fourth beast in Revelation 13:1 (NCV): "I saw a beast coming up out of the sea, having ten horns and seven heads." The book of Revelation presents vague references to the first, second, and third beast systems, namely, through the opening of the seals referenced in Revelation 6. However, Revelation contains extremely detailed insights into the fourth and fifth beast systems, signifying future events.

The book of Daniel provides a vivid description of the savage nature of the fourth beast: "it devoured and brake in pieces, and stamped the residue with its feet" (Dan. 7:7 ASV). The fourth beast leaves nothing but a wake of destruction and annihilates detractors. Daniel 7:8 (ASV) says that the fourth beast yields to a leader at a later point, a little horn, and "in this [little] horn were eyes like the eyes of a man, and a mouth speaking great things."

Today's symbolism for the New World Order frequently highlights the picture of an all-seeing eye. The all-seeing eye appears on the U.S. dollar bill atop a pyramid and featuring a phrase in Latin translated as "New Order of the Ages." The symbol is often associated with free masonry. The mainstream media could easily represent the "mouth speaking great things," tightly controlling the narrative globally. Over the past hundred years or more, media outlets consolidated to the point that they are owned by a handful of shareholders. Numerous compilations can easily be found online that show scores of media newscasters all reading from the same script, using the same word choices and nuanced emphasis. It would appear that tightly controlled news-media messaging goes forth worldwide, with newscasters actually directed on what to report in order to keep their jobs. The mouth of the fourth beast, the media, apparently shapes the public understanding of how the world "works" through a programmed narrative. Many people today adamantly refuse to accept any story not carried by the mainstream media, proving the effectiveness of the fourth beast's mouthpiece.

The Little Horn: Once an Entire Empire, Now an Invisible Hand

Of the ten horns or the nations of the fourth beast, three are subdued by a little horn. "Subdue" means "to subjugate, bring under control, to conquer." Three nations or kingdoms are controlled by the little horn. Daniel 7:8 (KJV) states "there came up...another little horn, before whom there were three of the first horns plucked up by the roots." Nations subdued by the little horn lose their foundation and instead become subjected to and directed by the little horn. The subdued nations are critical to the mission of the fourth beast, necessitating broader control. When I identified the nations today subdued by the little horn, I sadly recognized that they began with a noble cause, powerful charter, and ethical patriarchs. The subdued nations naively walked into masterful traps set by brilliant minds influenced by the master manipulator, Satan himself. Satan tempts people at their weakest points. For instance, Satan tempted Jesus at the end of His fast. Jesus overcame Satan's temptations three times despite bodily weakness following forty days of fasting.

Unfortunately, the three subdued nations failed their test. The little horn carefully waited for, or created, perfect moments of fragility within nations to seize control. By design, citizens and other followers of the subdued nations remained clueless, unaware of the leadership change.

So, who is the mysterious little horn wielding mighty influence through crafty subterfuge? We garner rich insight into the background and methods of the little horn in Daniel 11:21-24 (ASV):

> In his place shall stand up a contemptible person, to whom they had not given the honor of the kingdom, but he shall come in time of security and shall obtain the kingdom by flatteries. And the overwhelming forces shall be overwhelmed from before him, and shall be broken; yea, also the prince of the covenant. And after the league made with him he shall work deceitfully; for he shall come up, and shall become strong, with a small people. In a time of security shall he come even upon the fattest places of the province; and he shall do that which his fathers have not done, nor his fathers' fathers; he shall scatter among them prey, and spoil, and substance: yea, he shall devise his devices against the strongholds, even for a time.

The mysterious little horn inherits no legacy of royalty, meaning he does not originate from a royal family and does not possess a kingdom when he comes to power. Through manipulation and deceit, the little horn takes down governments, thus avoiding battlefield warfare. Instead, the takedown occurs during times of security or peace. The little horn achieves his objectives with a small people, meaning a tight-knit tribe of like-minded schemers versus a large army. The little horn overcomes kingdoms through flattery. Satan influenced the serpent and humans in the garden by promising them a higher status than their present situation. The same tactics are used by the little horn to influence leaders of nations. The little horn overwhelms and breaks the prince of the covenant. The word *covenant* is typically used in the context of God's covenant with Abraham, or when discussing the new covenant sealed with the blood of Jesus, both extremely powerful agreements with God. The little horn subdues an important religious leader, a prince of the covenant, who becomes part of the satanic leadership of the fourth beast. The passage indicates the little horn scatters prey, spoils, and substance. In other words, alignment with the little horn produces wealth for the subdued parties through bribes. The description and methods of the little horn in Daniel 11 clearly describe a small, severe, and shrewd race whose bloodline traces to modern ultra-elite power brokers.

The Little Horn: Masters of Infiltration and Control

I believe the little horn represents the descendants of the ancient tribe of Khazaria. Khazarians employed precisely the same tactics outlined in Daniel 11:21-24 to subdue nations, and their chosen symbolism and coat of arms remains consistent with fourth beast imagery described in the Bible. Although the Khazarians lost their empire to Russia in AD 1000, they skillfully utilized the art of behind-the-scenes political control in a highly effective manner which provides less possibility for military targeting. They masterfully integrated into the leadership of other societies and ultimately gained great power by operating behind-the-scenes. In one instance, the Khazars provided political asylum to the emperor Justinian

II of the Byzantine Empire (the Roman successor to the Roman Empire), who married a Khazar princess in AD 702. They also hosted Justinian II's rival Vardenes. A Byzantine-Khazar marriage alliance was arranged in which Constantine (later Constantine IV), Son of Leo, the Isaurian, married Cicek, the daughter of the Khagan in AD 730.[36] Their son, Leo IV (AD 775) the grandson of the Khazar sovereign, ascended the Byzantine throne as emperor and pope. Khazar troops were among the bodyguards of the Byzantine imperial court and fought for Leo IV against Simeon of Bulgaria. The Khazar leadership (the Khakan) was honored in diplomatic intercourse with the seal of three solidi, which marked him as a potente of the first rank, even above the pope and the Carolingian monarchs. So important to the Roman-Byzantines were the Khazars that the emperor Theophilus himself dispatched the materials and the workers to build for the Khazars a fortress impregnable to attack.[37] The Khazarian Jews integrated tightly with the Holy Roman Empire, the Roman successor to the Byzantine empire. The Khazarians likely founded the Jesuits, a powerful and militant order of the Catholic Church. Founder Ignatius of Loyola and his second in command and successor, Diego Laínez, were both Jewish converts and heavily funded by other Jewish converts. Many in the highest administrative offices in the early days of the Jesuits also were Jewish converts.[38]

The Khazarian coat of arms eerily depicts the image given to John in Revelation 13:2 (ASV), which describes the fourth beast, "The beast which I saw was like unto a leopard, and his feet were

---
36 *The Encyclopedia of Islam*, 4:1174.
37 Charles Norton Edgcumbe Eliot, "Khazars", *The Encyclopaedia Britannica*, 11th ed. (Cambridge, England: Cambridge University Press, 1911), 15:775.
38 Robert Aleksander Maryks, "Conclusion," in *The Jesuit Order as a Synagogue of Jews: Jesuits of Jewish Ancestry and Purity-of-Blood Laws in the Early Society of Jesus* (Leiden, Netherlands, Brill, 2010), xxii-xxiii, 215-18, www.jstor.org/stable/10.1163/j.ctt1w8h1xm.12.

as *the feet* of a bear, and his mouth as the mouth of the lion: and the dragon gave him his power, and his throne, and great authority." Figure 2 shows a picture of the early coat of arms of the Khazarians, complete with a cat body, lion's mouth, and bear claws for feet. The royal crown on the cat symbolizes kingship while the serpent tongue represents satanic control. Adding further context to this coat of arms is the picture in Daniel 7:7 (ASV) where the fourth beast "devoured and brake into pieces, and stamped the residue with its feet." The leopard in the coat of arms topples mountains (a symbol of leadership), cracks them, then stomps the cracked rock with its feet and claws.

Figure 2: *Khazarian Coat of Arms*

As the Khazarian tribe began to infiltrate and subdue other countries, they ultimately gained control of the world's banking and finance systems. A small number of families began to wield enormous power over the earth. Many of today's ultra-elites, including the Rothschilds, are most likely descendants of Khazaria. Leaders outside of America refer to this clan as the "Khazarian Mafia". Like the ancient Khazarians they pledged their allegiance to Satan, and he rewarded them with infinite wealth on the earth. However, Satan demanded their worship in return through a constant stream of child sacrifice and the relentless persecution and destruction of Christians. The practice of child sacrifice and Baal worship goes back to the ancient Babylonian kingdom, known as the first beast in the book of Daniel.

The little horn used its vast wealth and influence to subdue and control nations and purchased media empires to influence culture and demoralize nations. Abortion today actually represents a form of child sacrifice to the same satanic overlord, explaining the media's recent meltdown concerning the news of the overturning of Roe v. Wade, which legalized abortion at the federal level, in the Dobb's case. Satan possesses an insatiable desire for child sacrifice, as children are innocent before God. Destroying children is one way Satan fulfills his anger and hatred toward God. Satan also hates Christians, as evidenced by the extreme persecution of Christians worldwide. While Americans are mostly shielded from persecution, Christians in many parts of the world experience acute persecution and even death for their faith.

The fourth beast control system took two millennia to build, and nations did not succumb to the authority of the little horn overnight. The little horn gained more influence and power through control of the world financial system, and now it seems clear why certain nations were targeted to consolidate power. As a whole, the fourth beast exercises power and influence over virtually the entire earth. The little horn of the fourth beast systematically attacked nations of influence to achieve and maintain worldwide control. The little horn conquered three nations critical to controlling and perpetuating the fourth beast's dominion from a financial, military, and religious standpoint.

World Financial Control

Britain held the role of world financial center for a long time. At the end of the nineteenth century more than half the world's trade was executed in British currency. London, a hub for bankers and barons, benefited from extremely tight ties between the United Kingdom and the United States. The City of London, housing the primary central business district in London, incorporated as an independent state with its own charter. The Italian and Khazarian families who own the City of London invented the corporation, introducing the concept of liability protection.[39] These families were brilliant and savage chameleons, using assassination, blackmail, and bribes to achieve their goals. They settled in London and killed the rightful royal family in the seventeenth century at the hands of Oliver Cromwell, later subduing the throne with their own representative.[40] Britain soon became the launching pad for wars that expanded the reach of the British Empire. The British monarchy, subdued for the

---

[39] Larry Romanoff, "How the Khazarian-controlled City of London Was Set Up to Rule the World," *State of the Nation*, November 22, 2022, https://stateofthenation.co/?p=147524.

[40] Preston James, "The Hidden History of the Incredibly Evil Khazarian Mafia," *Veterans Today*, March 10, 2022, www.veteranstoday.com/2022/03/10 /the-hidden-history-of-the-incredibly-evil-khazarian-mafia

purposes of the fourth beast, became a vehicle of war to enrich its behind-the-scenes handlers.

The Rothschilds and Dutch House of Orange invented central banking when they founded the Bank of Amsterdam in the early 1600s.[41] The Bank of England followed, formed in 1694 by the Rothschilds and King William III, now related by marriage. This brilliant scheme allowed private central banks to print money in the name of a government and lend it back to the government with interest. The money is often traded for perceived value, with no backing of hard assets, commonly referred to as the "fiat money system" or "fractional reserve banking". The critical issue, actual ownership of the bank, determines the level of external control of a nation by the fourth beast. Countries operating a national central bank issuing their own currency, especially when backed by hard assets, control their own destiny. Nations that delegate the task of issuing currency to outside private interests become controlled by foreign interests.

The private central banking system dominates the world today. Private central banking allows a small group of banking families to control the world. Countries dependent on this system either execute the bidding of the private bankers or suffer the consequences. Over 95 percent of the world's countries utilize private central banks, each held by the Rothschild family and seven other prominent banking families.[42] The banks are named to mirror each country's name to lead people to believe that the bank is owned by the government of that country. Private central banking exists in the United States, under the name Federal Reserve Bank. The Federal Reserve Bank

---
41 Dean Henderson, *Big Oil and Their Bankers in the Persian Gulf: Four Horsemen, Eight Families & Their Global and Intelligence, Narcotics and Terror Network*, 3rd ed. (Scotts Valley, CA: CreateSpace, 2010), 307.
42 Dean Henderson, *The Federal Reserve Cartel* (self-published, 2005), chap. 1.

is neither federal (e.g., owned by the United States) nor does it possess real reserves. Since the early 1970s the Federal Reserve is not required to keep gold to back the U.S. dollar. U.S. dollars derive their value from perceived value alone.

In the United States two private central banks existed before the current Federal Reserve Bank. The First Bank of the United States was formed in 1791 by Alexander Hamilton and signed into law by George Washington, despite the opposition of Thomas Jefferson, who questioned the constitutionality of a private central bank.[43] Modeled after the Bank of England, the First Bank of the United States charter ended in 1811.[44] The Second Bank of the United States, chartered in 1816 by James Madison, suffered a similar fate in 1836. Andrew Jackson fought the private central bank during his election bid in 1832 and fulfilled his promise to kill the bank in 1836, despite an economic war with the private bank, which caused a depression by shrinking the money supply.[45] Jackson's actions made him an enemy of the bankers, and he survived an assassination attempt in 1835. Banking once again became decentralized in the United States.

The U.S. Civil War followed just over twenty years after the Second Bank of the United States failed to renew its charter. Grade school education teaches students the Civil War revolved strictly around slavery. Certainly, the U.S. founders missed a great opportunity by failing to abolish slavery in the U.S. Constitution. The evils of slavery are clear. There may be more to it, however. Otto von Bismark, the chancellor of Germany in the late 1800s, said:

---
[43] "Jefferson's Opinion on the Constitutionality of a National Bank: 1791," Yale Law School, accessed April 21, 2023, https://avalon.law.yale.edu/18th_century/bank-tj.asp.
[44] "The First Bank of the United States: A Chapter in the History of Central Banking," Federal Reserve Bank of Philadelphia, 2021, www.philadelphiafed.org/education/the-first-bank-of-the-united-states-a-chapter-in-the-history-of-central-banking.
[45] "Second Bank of the United States", *Wikipedia.org*, accessed April 21, 2023. https://en.wikipedia.org/wiki/Second_Bank_of_the_United_States.

The division of the United States into federations of equal force was decided long before the Civil War by the high financial powers of Europe. These bankers were afraid that the United States, if they remained in one block and as one nation, would attain economic and financial independence, which would upset their financial domination over the world. The voice of the Rothschilds prevailed...Therefore they sent their emissaries into the field to exploit the question of slavery and to open an abyss between the two sections of the Union.[46]

The sensational claim by Bismark that the Rothschilds fomented a color revolution to instigate the U.S. Civil War deserves further exploration. By the early 1860s the war effort depleted the Union's treasury and President Lincoln needed a solution. Lincoln convinced Congress to approve an emergency measure to allow the U.S. Treasury Department to print a new currency to fund the war, based on congressional power evident in the U.S. Constitution. While President Jackson formerly killed the private central bank, he failed to implement a replacement structure to prevent rogue currency. Lincoln organized a national banking scheme that worked beautifully. The war effort proceeded without foreign lending. In addition, the country's infrastructure dramatically improved.[47] The effort was short-lived; Lincoln's assassination in 1865 led to great compromise by his successors.

As time went on and bankers won additional allies, especially politicians, private central banking once again came to America. On

---

46 "Otto von Bismarck Quotes," accessed April 21, 2023, *AZQuotes.com*. https://www.azquotes.com/author/1426-Otto_von_Bismarck

47 Matthew Ehret, "How to Save a Dying Republic: Lincoln and the Greenbacks," August 29, 2021, Matthew Ehret (blog), accessed September 14, 2023. https://matthewehret.substack.com/p/how-to-save-a-dying-republic-lincoln.

Christmas Eve 1913 the Federal Reserve Act of 1913 was signed into law by President Woodrow Wilson. The Act officially took the power to create money away from Congress and the U.S. Treasury and handed it back to the private bankers in a charter with no expiration date. This development represented a major victory for the Rothschilds and other participating banking families. The last real attempt to change this system was made by John F. Kennedy in the 1960s, through the introduction of silver-backed currency, but this was followed shortly by Kennedy's assassination. The United States officially once again yielded to the fourth beast system.

World Military Control

The United States operates the most powerful military in the world. Despite being founded on Godly principles with freedoms codified in the Declaration of Independence, the Constitution, and the Bill of Rights, the United States remains an important element of the fourth beast system. Since the signing of the Federal Reserve Act of 1913, the United States fought numerous wars on behalf of the fourth beast, beginning with World War I. Many invaded nations printed their own money before the United States attacked but immediately installed a private central bank once conquered. Today it's not just the bankers benefiting – Washington, DC is driven by a powerful military-industrial complex eager to keep the machine running. Washington would appear to find war irresistible. Washington recently gave more than $100 billion in aid to Ukraine, the birthplace of the Khazarian empire, and as of yet the aid remains unaudited. There are many patriots in the United States and the spirit of freedom runs deep, however, U.S. leadership and its control structure would appear to remain influenced and controlled by the fourth beast.

World Religious Control

The Catholic Church ascribes its roots to the apostle Peter, a member of the inner circle of Jesus. However, Catholicism was actually born out of a merger of Rome and Christianity, retaining pagan symbolism that Peter would not have condoned. The Catholic Church amassed considerable wealth by the eighteenth century. The Treaty of Paris of 1763 designated British King George III Arch-Treasurer and Prince Elector of the Holy Roman Empire. By this time the Rothschilds already controlled the British crown, and according to the *Encyclopedia Judaica* the Rothschilds bear the title Guardians of the Vatican Treasury.[48] A rift existed between the Jesuit Order, the militant arm of the Catholic Church, and the pope, who at that time did not want to acknowledge the Jesuit Order. To regain power, the Jesuits began the Bavarian Illuminati with one of their soldiers, Adam Weishaupt.[49] The Rothschilds eagerly backed Weishaupt and formed an alliance with the Jesuits that continues to the present day. The alliance between the Jesuits and the Rothschilds later extended to the Morgans and Rockefellers, chiefly to pull down constitutional liberty in America and bring the pope to world domination.[50] Ultimately, many people are tempted by power. Satan, desiring world domination, remains impartial to the methods, people or institutions required to achieve his goal. He wants to be on the winning team. Satan lies to his subjects,

---
48 F. Tupper Saussy, *Rulers of Evil* (n.p.: Ospray, 1999), 160-61.
49 Eric Jon Phelps, *Vatican Assassins*, 2nd ed.(n.p.: Halcyon, 2001), 582.
50 Bill Hughes, *The Secret Terrorists* (city: Truth Triumphant, 2002), 16-17.

promising them he, not God, wins. The wealthy and influential are targets, especially those with insatiable greed.

Today, there are nearly one billion followers within the Catholic Church. Videos have surfaced of Pope Francis and other church leaders bowing to ultra-wealthy globalist leaders. At some point in Catholic Church history, the church's institutional leadership fell to the little horn and is now also part of the fourth beast system. There are millions of faithful and believing Catholics in the world. Many devoted Catholics love Jesus and are born-again believers. However, the leadership of the Catholic Church is subdued and taken over. More recently, Pope Francis repeated verbatim the wishes of globalist lords within the World Economic Forum, a clear sign that the Catholic Church remains under the control of the fourth beast.[51] The papacy enjoys a unique role in the world: the pope is invited to virtually every nation as a spiritual leader. It makes sense for the power and influence of the Vatican to be chosen by Satan as a tool of influence. Today, the Vatican is considered sovereign territory not subject to local Italian laws, just as the City of London and Washington D.C. also are considered sovereign.

Severe judgment will come to the Roman Catholic Church – it allowed itself to be subdued by the fourth beast while purporting to proclaim the gospel as the purveyor of truth. In Revelation 17, we learn of the great harlot of Babylon. The harlot is linked to the fourth beast system, as indicated by the reference to the ten horns and seven kings. In the Bible, harlotry is how the Lord refers to Israel's faithless relationship whenever Israel chose to follow idols rather than simply worshiping the Lord. Christianity steeped in idolatry represents the new form of harlotry. The clothing of the harlot in

---

51   Gary Kah, "Pope Francis: Facilitating the Globalist Agenda," Gary H. Kah (blog), accessed June 6, 2023, https://garykah.org/pope-francis-facilitating-the-globalist-agenda.

Revelation 17:4 is purple and red, the color for Catholic bishops and cardinals, respectively.[52] The Catholic Church, pretends to be the true church, but it is really based on the Babylonian rooted religion of sun and Satan worship.[53] The Catholic Church leaders would seem to be compromised by the fourth beast. However, there are many devoted Catholics, most of whom truly love God and are followers of Jesus.

The Bible foretold of the Church's alignment with the fourth beast system ages ago. In Daniel 2:33 the Bible describes the fourth beast comprising ten toes, some iron and some clay. The iron represents the government. The clay represents the Church. The alliance between government and church was prophesied thousands of years ago. Daniel 2:34 foretells a stone made without hands smashing the image on his feet so that the statue representing the four beasts becomes dust. This stone made without hands shows judgment is executed by God directly. No single person will get the credit for destroying the fourth beast system, for it is God who gets the glory. You don't want to be involved with the fourth beast system when this happens.

Modern Fourth Beast Symbolism

The model of subduing nations comprising the fourth beast system is an ancient strategy. Satan uses brilliant minds and trickery to manipulate circumstances for a desired outcome, exactly like he did in Genesis 3 when he subdued the serpent. Satan marks his territory through symbolism. The Vatican, the City of London, and

---

52 Peter M. J. Stravinskas, ed. *Our Sunday Visitor's Catholic Encyclopedia* (Huntington, IN: Our Sunday Visitor, 1991), 175, 178, 466.
53 David Nikao Wilcoxson, "Revelation 17 – The Harlot Roman Catholic Church," *Revelation Timeline Decoded*, accessed June 6, 2023, https://revelationtimelinedecoded.com/revelation-17-the-harlot-roman-catholic-church

Washington, DC all display signature symbolism of the fourth beast system. Roman architectural influence evidences the government buildings located in these three cities. The City of London features a phallic-shaped obelisk called Cleopatra's Needle, relocated from the ruins of the Caesareum of Alexandria in the nineteenth century.[54] Washington, DC, features the largest obelisk, the Washington Monument. The Vatican features an Egyptian obelisk, taken from Egypt by the ancient Romans. St. Peter's Square shares the same geographic pinpoint as the Circus of Nero, where Emperor Nero executed St. Peter and other Christians.[55] Near the Pentagon stands a chilling Air Force Memorial with three enormous, wicked horns. The Pentagon building shape closely relates to the ancient satanic pentagram, and the streets of Washington, DC are also pentagon shaped. The area around the U.S. Capitol is owl shaped, a creature worshiped by the ancient Khazarians. The Capitol is crowned with a statue of Roman goddess Persephone, who rules the dead and all else that is within the earth, namely metals and precious stones.[56] Hundreds of pages would be required to fully document the ancient Roman and Babylonian symbolism contained within Washington, DC, Rome, and the City of London. The symbolism is not coincidental or accidental. In the same way Satan subdued the serpent in the garden, the ablest creature in its day, he chose to tempt and subdue the ablest and most influential nations. Citizens or followers of these nations are given the illusion of control. However, the fix is in at the top.

---

54 "Cleopatra's Needle," accessed April 24, 2023, *Wikipedia.org*, https://en.wikipedia.org/wiki/Cleopatra%27s_Needle,_London.
55 Jimmy Kennedy, "The Story of the Vatican Obelisk," December 28, 2021, *Vatican Tips* (blog), https://vaticantips.com/vatican-obelisk.
56 F. Tupper Saussy, *Rulers of Evil: Useful Knowledge About Governing Bodies* (Santa Monica, CA: Osprey, 2001), 234

The Family Crest: A Picture of the Fourth Beast

The coat of arms of the Rothschild family, shareholders in the world's private central banks, provides incredible insight into the power structure of the fourth beast (see Fig. 3). Recognizable on the left of the coat of arms is the leopard body with a lion's mouth and bear feet, similar to the early coat of arms of the Khazarian tribe, and described in Revelation 13:2. However, the crown is now represented by three battle crowns. The leftmost crown represents the Vatican, symbolized by the star of the sea, an early representation of Mary, the mother of Jesus. On the left crown we also see a serpent missing both its head and tail, symbolizing total subjection. *Vatican* literally means divining serpent. The middle battle crown represents the United States, as symbolized by an eagle. The third battle crown represents the British crown, as symbolized by blue and white plumes, the original colors of the British crown. Opposite the leopard we see a sinister pale white horse with a single horn. The white horse is the first of the seven seals opened in Revelation 6:2, which represents the ancient Chaldean-Babylonian Empire (not to be confused with the white horse Jesus rides in Revelation 19). The Babylonian Empire is the root of the beast system, the head of the body in the dream of King Nebuchadnezzar in Daniel 2. Human sacrifice, including children, a staple ritual during the entire existence of Babylon, carried through each beast system. Today child sacrifice is either underground or accomplished by government-sanctioned abortion. The white horse also represents false religion, and the unicorn horn represents magic. Note both the leopard and the unicorn have serpent tongues, indicating satanic leadership and reptilian seed. In the crest are two powerful arms clutching tightly a total of ten arrows representing ten nations of the fourth beast system. Three words are written at the bottom. *Concordia* is the name of the ancient Roman goddess of peace. *Industria* is Latin for labor. *Integritas* is Latin for integrity. The symbolism of this coat of arms is a complete representation of the fourth beast imagery described in the Bible, down to the smallest detail.

Figure 3: *Rothschild Family Coat of Arms*

World Control Through the Finance System

Revelation 13:7 (NLT) says, "The beast was allowed to wage war against God's holy people and to conquer them. And he was given authority to rule over every tribe and people and language and nation." The private central banking system, controlled by the banking families, exists in all but three countries in the world today. The management of each country's pocketbook wields unprecedented control or authority. By controlling the money supply the bankers exercise near total control of a nation. Shrinking the money supply produces recession, and expanding the money supply produces bubbles and inflation. The Rothschilds and their allies control each government at the macrolevel. Control of the private central banking system, attained by war, assassinations, and backroom deals, forced nearly every nation into a system of debt control. The total authority prophesied in Revelation 13:7 is fulfilled. So, how do nonbelievers worship the fourth beast? Faith in government or money as a more reliable source than God constitutes worship in the sight of God. The money we so diligently work for is not worth the paper it's written on.

Today we carry paper notes that represent our money, typically lacking any backing of hard assets. While the fourth beast fooled the people, he confiscated true wealth. The Bible points out that the fourth beast and specifically the little horn controls the world's precious metals and other valuable commodities. Daniel 11:43 (MSG) states, "He will confiscate the treasuries of Egyptian gold and silver and other valuables. The Libyans and Ethiopians will fall in with him." In modern language the last part of this verse could be translated as "and the Arab and African nations will obey him." As discussed, nearly the whole world obeys him. Gold and silver are real wealth for all of recorded history. The once world-ruling Egyptians transferred all their wealth to the Israelites when Moses led them from Egypt, including their gold, silver, and other precious possessions. Daniel makes it clear the world's resources are controlled by the little horn through confiscation. Today only a handful of families control the world's precious metals and natural resources.

How Long Does the Fourth Beast Rule?

Each beast kingdom mentioned in Daniel 7 possessed dominion. The word *dominion* means "sovereignty" or "rule." *Dominion* also means "possessing mastery" or "authority to rule." God showed Daniel that each of the four beasts possessed a time of dominion or rule, with both a beginning and an end. The time of dominion compares to a real-estate lease. After a tenant's lease ends, the tenant returns the property back to the owners. For better or worse, God showed Daniel several evil beast systems would rule for extended periods in the geopolitical realm. I believe people's mistakes and disobedience allowed Satan to rule for extended periods.

Numerous references in Scripture set the term of the lease of the fourth beast. References in both Daniel (7:25; 12:7) and Revelation (12:14) mention "a time, two times, half a time" to describe the length of time the fourth beast rules. I believe most scholars incorrectly interpret this to mean three and a half years. However, I believe the reference means 2,150 years. To explain, *times* equals 1,000 years (two times equals 2,000 years), while *time* equals 100 years, and *half a time* equals 50 years. Based on when the Roman Empire began, we are nearing or perhaps already reached the end of the fourth beast lease. Many debate precisely when the Roman Empire began, marking the start of the fourth beast system. While Rome defeated Greece in 146 BC, they did not fully consolidate power until later. There are signs today indicating the decline of the fourth beast has already begun; Large swaths of humanity are becoming aware of the tactics and methods of the fourth beast system. This points to the decline of the fourth beast, which has operated under the cloak of secrecy until now. In the near future the fourth beast will die. There are Soldier Saints who are more awake than the general public praying against the fourth beast and using methods remarkably similar to Cyrus, who conquered ancient Babylon from within, through subterfuge and special operations. The plans are in place for the death and destruction of the fourth beast, all orchestrated by God through a supernatural miracle only He could accomplish.

Satanic Little Horn: Type and Shadow of the Anti-Christ

The number forty-two appears in the Bible on numerous occasions. God forced unfaithful Israel to wander the desert forty-two times in forty years before given rest (Num. 33). When a group of men began to mock the anointed prophet Elisha, he cursed them, and two large female bears came out of the woods and tore forty-two of them to pieces (2 Kings 2:24). Forty-two is often found as a factor in anti-Christian names, such as Nimrod.[57] Jewish scholars point out in the Hebrew language, *mem* (forty) and *bet* (two) are also the first letter of the Torah and the Oral Torah, representing a unification of the two.[58] Earlier in this chapter, I discussed how the oral tradition (rabbinical commentary) of the scholars and elders concerning Jewish life actually presents a "perversion of faith" according to Jesus.

The most well-known use of the number forty-two in the Bible relates to the coming anti-Christ, who tramples on the holy city for forty-two months (Rev 11:1-2). However, the little horn, the

---

[57] "Meaning of Numbers in the Bible: The Number 42," *Biblestudy.org*, accessed June 8, 2023, www.biblestudy.org/bibleref/meaning-of-numbers-in-bible/42.html.

[58] Hillel ben David, "The Significance of The Number Forty-Two (42)," *betamunah.org*, accessed June 8, 2023, www.betemunah.org/fortytwo.html

satanic overlord of the fourth beast, also acts with great authority for forty-two months (Rev 13:5). These two Scriptures cause many to confuse the anti-Christ with the little horn, but *they are different.* The anti-Christ is a person who rules the world during the Great Tribulation, just before the battle of Armageddon. The anti-Christ is the *fifth* beast, not the fourth. The little horn represents a tribe that over many generations subdues nations to gain control of the fourth beast. While Satan controls both the little horn and the anti-Christ, they appear in different ages in the Bible.

A month contains a collection of typically thirty days, and in the Bible a day can equal a year (Num. 14:33-34; Ezek. 4:4-6) or a thousand years (2 Pet. 3:8). I believe the forty-two months of control by the little horn represents 1,260 years of great authority during the time of the fourth beast, a shadow of the forty-two *actual* months (three and a half years) full reign of the anti-Christ during the Great Tribulation. Forty-two months equals 1,260 years, assuming each day equals a year. To explain, 42 months times 30 days per month equals 1,260. While the fourth beast's geopolitical lease on earth lasts 2,150 years, full authority lasts 1,260 years. Revelation 13:5 (YLT) says, "There was given to it a mouth speaking great things, and evil-speakings, and there was given to it authority to make war forty-two months." This reference follows the description of the *fourth* beast in Revelation 13:1. A few verses later in Revelation, we are introduced to the fifth beast, the anti-Christ, "Then I saw *another* beast come up out of the earth...He exercised all the authority of the first beast. And he required all the earth and its people to worship the first beast, whose *fatal wound* had been healed" (Rev 13:11-12 NLT, emphasis added). The fatal wound refers to the brutal death of the fourth beast at the end of the times of the Gentiles, the stone judgment. Given the Khazarian Empire's rise to power in the eighth and ninth centuries, or roughly 1,250 years ago, the forty-two months could indicate the time frame of full satanic control of the fourth beast system by the Khazarian cabal.

Consolidation of Power: The New World Order

The satanic consolidation of power through the banking system and the merger with both perverted Christianity and perverted Judaism produced a globalist cabal with a lust for world domination. From early Rome's brutal reign to the Spanish Inquisitions to the hundreds of wars over the past two centuries, the fourth beast ruled with bloodshed. Under the fourth beast dominion, Satan attempted through various campaigns to enforce world rule. In the nineteenth and twentieth centuries, through the private banking systems and numerous wars, consolidation of power and extreme genocide accelerated. The cabal attempted to force world rule in 1918 via the League of Nations' plan to erase national sovereignty. This premature plan failed when the people revolted. Brutal dictators soon followed, including Stalin and Mao, who pushed murderous communism on their countries, leading to the deaths of over 100 million people. Hitler possessed a vision of world control and failed. The Khazarians used their influence with Stalin, Mao, and Hitler, initially. It would unfortunately appear that we are closer than ever in modern times to experiencing a one-world satanic government. Many world leaders currently speak the same language, specifically referring to the "New World Order". Using terms like *sustainability* and *saving the environment*, monsters disguised in pressed suits push the same tired satanic agenda of one-world rule. The United Nations introduced Agenda 2030, which claims, "Population growth is one of the most serious obstacles to world prosperity and sustainable development," contrary to God's abundance blessing to humanity in Genesis 1:20, when He directed us to "be fruitful and multiply".[59] The names, terminology, and methods change, but history repeats itself as Satan once again tries to push his agenda to kill, steal and destroy.

1800 to Present: Extreme Genocide

As the fourth beast consolidated power in the last two centuries, mass genocide accelerated in terms of sheer body count. The fourth beast became a highly efficient death machine, producing exponentially more death and destruction in the last two hundred years than in the past two thousand years. The following are just a few examples:

- 1 billion babies aborted since 1920[60]

- 183 to 311 million deaths related to war and war-related famine across 120 wars (note the number of deaths exceeded all wars in the prior two thousand years)[61]

- 125 million deaths from famine since 1860[62]

- 100 million-plus cancer deaths, a relatively new disease beginning in the twentieth century

---

59 "Report of the International Conference on Population and Development," United Nations, Cairo, Egypt, September 5-13, 1994, 173.
60 W. Robert Johnston and Thomas Jacobsen, *Abortion Worldwide Report: 100 Nations, 1 Century, 1 Billion Babies*, (Colorado Springs, CO: GLC, 2017).
61 "List of Wars by Death Toll," *Wikipedia.org*, accessed June 7, 2023, https://en.wikipedia.org/wiki/List_of_wars_by_death_toll.
62 "Food and Agriculture," *Our World in Data*, accessed June 20, 2023, https://ourworldindata.org/famines.

- 80 million deaths in communist China[63]
- 66 million, mostly Christians, murdered in Russia by the communist Bolsheviks[64]

Adding an additional 200 to 270 million deaths from wars fought from the time of ancient Rome to about AD 1800 brings the death total to between 1.9 and 2.1 billion deaths. Using a conservative estimate of a current world population of 8 billion people, about 25 percent of humanity was destroyed under the fourth beast, a fulfillment of prophecy. The Bible aptly labeled the fourth beast the pale horse in Revelation 6:8 (MSG), stating, "I looked. A colorless horse, sickly pale. Its rider was Death, and Hell was close on its heels. They were given power to destroy a fourth of the earth by war, famine, disease, and wild beasts." The Bible's prophetic warning concerning the destruction of 25 percent of humankind by the fourth beast is a solemn warning. The methods of death indicated in Revelation 6:8 include war, famine, disease, and wild beasts. I consider the doctors willing to perform abortions upon defenseless, innocent children to be wild beasts. In some forms of abortion the baby is torn limb from limb while still alive and without any sedation, a truly barbaric way to die.

New World Order: Destined to Fail

Despite the best efforts by powerful forces to institute a satanic world government, the plan always fails according to Scripture. Satan tried numerous times to achieve his goal of a one-world satanic government. Satan's track record of success is dismal. He failed to

---

[63] Valerie Strauss and Daniel Southerl, "How Many Died? New Evidence Suggests Far Higher Numbers for the Victims of Mao Zedong's Era," *Washington Post*, July 17, 1994.
[64] Alexander Solzhenitsyn, *Gulag Archipelago Two* (1918-1956) (New York: Harper & Row, 1975), 10.

overcome prophecy when attempting to destroy Moses, the deliverer of Israel. Through Herod, he tried once again to divine prophecy and destroy the infant Jesus. However, God's Word always prevails. Satan is simply a fallen created being unable to overcome His Creator, the Scriptures or the Biblical timetable. Satan fails repeatedly each and every time he attempts to overthrow God. All the prophecies related to the fourth beast are fulfilled. His time is running short. Believer's must heed the call when God says to "cast out demons in My name" (Mark 16:17 NLT).

5. Learning to Fight Back

The kings of the earth prepare to fight, and their leaders make
plans together against the Lord and his appointed one.
They say, "Let's break the chains that hold us back
and throw off the ropes that tie us down."
But the one who sits in heaven laughs;
the Lord makes fun of them.
– Ps. 2:2-4 NCV

When I first understood we live in the time of the fourth beast, it occurred to me that Jesus also walked the earth during the same age. It's humbling to recognize we live in the same beast system Jesus endured during His ministry on earth. How did Jesus handle it? He recognized all the enemies' tactics and refused to live in fear. Despite nervous rumblings from the Romans about the growing influence of Jesus' ministry or threats from the Pharisees, Jesus operated with immunity until He gave Himself to die to save humanity. We can emulate Jesus today and learn to fight back. We also learn from Jesus how to recognize all the enemies' tactics and shed naive ideas surrounding the operations of our enemy.

Jesus provided the best example for today's Soldier Saints to see through the veneer. We are to follow Jesus' example, recognize enemy assignments, and refuse to let them into our sacred circles of marriage, family, and business. If we understand the big picture, we know what to do when a "friendly destroyer" shows up in our lives. Be very cautious regarding allowing the world's technology, banking, and finance system to control your personal life or your business. Later, I discuss the perils of debt slavery on the lives of Christians. As a parent, I am also aware of traps that are laid for children at various stages of development. My own son became hooked on the video game Roblox, which quickly became an addiction and drew him away from God. Roblox's sign up screen, "Sign up and start having fun" *seemed* so benign, so innocent. You see, Satan wants us to entertain idols of any sort, to pull us away from God. He really does not care what method sticks. It could be pornography, sports, career – anything that we put in front of God. We must recognize the traps and pass the test, staying close to God for strength and discernment. Jesus provides the ultimate example. Before Jesus performed a single miracle or launched into public ministry, God led Him to the desert to overcome temptation. God's only son needed to demonstrate that He could see through the enemy's devices – do you think God expects less from us? All Soldier Saints go through the same testing ground – it starts with small things. When Jesus went to the desert for His testing ground, the crowds weren't there. But God knew what needed to come first before launching Jesus' ministry into the public arena.

How Did Jesus Deal with Rome?

While He lived in the time of the fourth beast, Jesus exercised complete authority over the spiritual realm. He cast out devils, healed the sick, and performed miracles. However, Jesus did not attempt to master the geopolitical realm. He did not overthrow Rome and save the Judeans from the Roman overlords. His inaction on the geopolitical front confused the Judeans because they thought the Messiah would rule and reign politically, not spiritually. Jesus expressed no interest in reigning politically but instead focused on spiritual deliverance and salvation of the people. Jesus brought the spiritual reunification of humans with God, not political peace. Jesus likely studied the book of Daniel and knew the fourth beast's reign continued for a couple thousand more years, and He did not bother to change the system before the preset time.

While the saint's official time of geopolitical rule occurs a couple of millennia after Jesus' ministry on earth, the Bible did not instruct saints to remain passive. In 1 Timothy 2:2 (NLT) Paul commands us to "Pray...for kings and all who are in authority so that we can live peaceful and quiet lives marked by godliness and dignity." We are commanded to pray for our leaders so *we* experience times of peace while *we* fulfill God's call on our lives. Regardless of whether our leaders are infiltrated and controlled by the fourth beast, we pray for them so we can do God's work in peace. I don't believe this applies to illegitimate leaders. If a democratic leader comes to power illegally (e.g., contrary to the vote of the people), we shouldn't pray for this leader, but rather for justice. In the same way that the prophets knew God anointed David as his king, not Adonijah, we should know who to support and pray for. Jesus also commanded in Luke 19:13 (KJV), "Occupy till I come." This command means to take possession – an active concept. We take possession of our allotted domains. Our instruction in Daniel 11:32 (NKJV), a direct reference to the time of the fourth beast, nails it: "Those who do wickedly against the covenant he [the little horn, which controls the fourth beast] shall corrupt with flattery; but the people who know their God shall be strong, and carry out great exploits." In other words, despite the fourth beast control system, saints who dare to believe and are strong in faith and courageous are rewarded by God and carry out exploits.

There are numerous examples in modern history of saints who exploit. Men and women who fearlessly choose to trust God and have great faith are rewarded. It is possible to overcome the system in the face of near complete control on the other end. For example, despite the best efforts to quench the Church by Satan over the last couple thousand years, nearly 700 million Spirit-filled Pentecostal Christians are present on earth today, up from almost none at the turn of the twentieth century.[65] Called and driven missionaries helped fuel the growth of charismatic believers, despite enduring personal danger. God always finds a way to reach those hungry for Him.

Recognize the Cabal

Jesus remained immune from the threat of crucifixion until He challenged the money changers. He regularly agitated the Pharisees by healing on the Sabbath and giving His disciples permission to pick grain on the Sabbath. Jesus seemed to enjoy upending the religious order of the day. Scripture points out the Pharisees sought ways to destroy Jesus, but they feared the people, many of whom

---

[65] See, for example, Todd Johnson and Gina A. Zurlo, *Spirit-Empowered Christianity: Global Pentecostalism in the 21st Century* (Tulsa, OK: Oral Roberts University Press, 2020).

followed Jesus. In the same way He stood up to the religious leaders, Jesus confronted the political leaders. In Luke 13:31 (AMPC) the Pharisees, presumably speaking for Herod, the pro-Roman ruler, told Him "Go away from here, for Herod is determined to kill you." In the next verse Jesus responded by telling them, "Go and tell that fox, Behold I drive out demons and perform healings today and tomorrow, and on the third day I finish My course." The Greek term *fox* implies one who is, "sly and crafty, skulking and cowardly" – hardly an endearing term. Even after His boldness toward Herod, the Jews lacked the political capital to destroy Jesus. It came to a head when Jesus went after the money changers (bankers in today's terminology). In Matthew 21 just before His crucifixion, Jesus cleaned out the temple and overthrew the money changers. This mysterious group of bankers flexed political muscle both with Rome and among the religious leaders, who both likely profited off their trade.

The money changers likely held no leadership positions in the synagogues. They quietly conducted their trade in the temple, meaning at some point these bankers convinced the Jewish leaders into allowing them to conduct their trade. Kickbacks or bribes likely went to the chief priest to look the other way. The money changers likely cornered the market on the temple money supply, which gave them complete control over currency trade. As vast numbers of worshipers poured into the temple from around the world, foreign currency needed to be exchanged into acceptable temple currency, for a fee of course. Not wanting to miss out on another market, it's apparent this group expanded into the sale of doves and other acceptable animal sacrifices. To exist separately from the existing Roman currency, the temple economy likely persisted through kickbacks to the Roman authorities. Jesus threatened this business by overturning their tables, impacting both the Jews and the Romans financially. Shortly after Jesus worked to cleanse the temple of the moneychangers, the Jews possessed the political capital to crucify Jesus, part of the divine plan all along.

In His ministry, Jesus criticized the Pharisees and the Jewish leaders of the day. He repeatedly warned His disciples not to fall into the trap of judging based on the law or putting tradition above human needs. He seemed to relish the Sabbath as another opportunity to make the Pharisees' heads explode. He disparaged Herod, the pro-Roman Jewish king, who held office amid scandalous circumstances. However, He also taught about another group more subtle than either the Jews or the Romans, the satanic invisible hand of the fourth beast, who controlled both the Jews and Rome.

Spot the Traps

In Matthew 10:16 (NLT) Jesus told His disciples to be "shrewd as snakes and harmless as doves." In Genesis 3:1 (AMPC), the serpent possessed skills "more subtle *and* crafty than any living creature of the field which the Lord God had made." The serpent's seed would one day do battle with Jesus, and Jesus would crush the serpent's head. Jesus implored His disciples to be as wise as a serpent, essentially educating and commanding them to operate at the same level of cunning as the reptilian seed without losing the grace of their calling. In Mark 16:18 (NLT), as a final command to His followers, Jesus said, "They will be able to handle snakes with safety, and if they drink anything poisonous, it won't hurt them." Jesus is showing His disciples their authority to handle the serpent class and even be immune from intentional poisoning or other traps by the serpent class. In Luke 10:19, He said as well, "Look, I have given you authority over all the power of the enemy, and you can walk among snakes and scorpions and crush them. Nothing will injure you."

These passages remind me again of the prophet Daniel, the senior adviser of several Babylonian and Persian kings. Daniel walked among the leaders, and kings listened to his wisdom, allowing Daniel to protect his people at critical junctures. We need more Christians today walking among snakes and scorpions! I know patriots regularly attending the Davos World Economic Forum – they are there on a divine mission among snakes and scorpions. Jesus called out the serpent influence among the Pharisees in Matthew 23:33 (NCV), "You are snakes! A family of poisonous snakes! How are you going to escape God's judgment?" Why such an emphasis on serpents? The satanic overlords run the various beast systems. Jesus taught His disciples about taking authority over this realm and even walking among the serpents and escaping traps; they enjoyed supernatural protection.

The Sons of the Age

In the same way, Jesus taught His disciples through parables regarding the spirit of mammon, the political currency of the fourth beast. In a strange Scripture, Jesus says, "Use your worldly resources to benefit others and make friends. Then, when your possessions are gone, they will welcome you to an eternal home" (Luke 16:9 NLT). This verse falls directly after He told the parable describing a lazy, incompetent person on the verge of getting fired who proceeded to give gifts to others by stealing from his master to save his own skin. Jesus said the master, upon discovering the self-serving nature of the servant, *praised* the dishonest manager for acting shrewdly and prudently. Then Jesus makes a profound statement, "The sons of this age are shrewder *and* more prudent *and* wiser in their own generation than are the sons of light" (Luke 16:8 AMPC). The sons of this age are the sovereigns that rule the fourth beast system. Jesus is warning His people to wake up and understand their system. Jesus implored His followers to acquire shrewd wisdom and operate at a higher level of awareness. The dishonest manager stole from his master to save his own skin, and his master thought him wise for doing so. Today's Christians would judge the servant as sneaky and his master as incompetent, missing the whole point of Jesus' lesson. In modern jargon, Jesus told His followers to wake up and smell the coffee. The overlords of this age exercise mastery over their system; don't judge but rather understand and respect it.

How does this lesson apply today? Be aware of the methods used by the fourth beast overlords to acquire and keep their power. Know the fourth beast system involves blackmail, bribes, cheating, stealing, and mind control. The fourth beast finds those with wealth and with followers and seeks to control and manipulate them through influence, blackmail, or theft. As saints acquire wealth or influence, they also become targets. The fourth beast uses a nation's tax dollars against its citizens and plunders natural resources for its own purposes. We must recognize when the fourth beast is attempting to numb our senses through television, sports, fake news, and celebrity gossip. Don't get caught up in the prevailing system and lose focus on God's plan for our lives. Don't be naive – be wise as serpents and harmless as doves. We need to win despite the fourth beast system. Winning requires supernatural wisdom and shrewd, worldly understanding.

Years ago, after building a successful business, I was approached by a man who wanted to invest. Up to then I spent an inordinate amount of time fundraising, and this gentleman offered to alleviate the burden of fundraising by providing a loan with easy terms. This man gave my wife the creeps. Ignoring my wife's instinct, I accepted the loan and soon began having trouble with my new lending partner. The evil assignment nearly succeeded in wiping me out. The Holy Spirit desires that we walk in a place of spiritual sensitivity so we avoid these situations. Men in particular sometimes struggle to identify others' character. It's wise to heed our marriage partner's instincts and spend time praying before we covenant with others. Today, I live a debt-free life and purpose to stay that way.

Determine to be shrewd; otherwise, we get beat. While saints slumbered, the fourth beast system took over schools, elections, and Congress. Our rapture paralysis and insular mentality kept us from fighting back. Be aware of the battle prophesied thousands of years ago through Daniel. He says that the fourth beast "will speak words against the Most High, and he will wear out the holy ones of the Most High" (Dan. 7:25 LEB). Other translations say the fourth beast is cruel to the saints. *Merriam-Webster* defines *wear out* as "to make useless especially by long or hard usage." *Wiktionary* defines it this way: "to deteriorate or become unusable or ineffective due to continued strain – to exhaust, to cause or contribute to fatigue or weariness." These definitions imply the fourth beast uses our own life, stamina, and resources for its purpose to the point where we are used up and ineffective.

How to Beat The System

In the prior chapter I covered the extreme genocide that occurred in the last two hundred years. Wars, famine, and pestilence, trademarks of the fourth beast system, continue to wear out the saints. Christian persecution continues to reach new, historic levels on a worldwide basis. However, the fourth beast uses other, more subtle methods to wear out the saints. The following examples articulate a number of other methods and practical ways to beat the system:

1. Tax dollars. The fourth beast is a system of nations (governments) building an apparatus of control. The fourth beast takes our tax money and uses it to build governing agencies designed to infiltrate our lives to stamp out our vigor, freedom, and faith. For example, the Department of Education, established in the late 1970s under President Jimmie Carter, arguably achieved little to advance education. On the contrary, the Department of Education used our money to introduce sex education, godless curriculum, critical race theory, and other ideas that dumb down and confuse our children. After the formation of the Department of Education, did Christians protest a new agency designed to corrupt our children? Christians need to question and challenge government programs and demand reform by our elected leaders. We should also explore legal loopholes to minimize or *eliminate* our tax bills.

2. Foundations and corporate charities. The Ford Foundation began with a wealthy family leading with character. However, agents of the fourth beast system infiltrated the Ford Foundation (as well as many others), so that today billions of dollars are spent each year by subdued foundations and other like-minded organizations to demoralize our society. Many don't understand the sheer amount of coordination involved in

Learning to Fight Back

directing funds. Researchers documented the flow of these funds and organizations participating in demoralizing America. Their methodology centered on which secular, religious and media organizations regularly accept money from foundations known to promote the destruction of America. Figure 4 highlights well-known foundations, corporations, and, unfortunately, Christian-based organizations now part of the system to destroy and demoralize the American public. The Engine of Harm outlined in Figure 4 details well-funded specific projects designed to weaken America and her Christian faith. To access a more detailed chart displaying over one hundred well-known organizations participating in the engine of harm, visit revelationriddle.com.

Figure 4: *Engine of Harm*[66]

While Figure 4 highlights orchestrated efforts to undermine and demoralize America, similar orchestration exists in other

---

66   Derived from a wide variety of documents available in the public domain.

nations. Saints need to understand donations to seemingly benign causes often get used for harmful purposes. Pay attention to charitable causes you support – a small donation on a grocery store checkout screen may be directed to nefarious causes.

3. Church infiltration. Virtually every Christian denomination started with a fresh insight from God or a specific revival. Affected communities began to meet around a powerful common cause, inspired to build buildings and infrastructure to support their assemblies. Sadly, today, many churches are shells of their former glory, slowly shedding members due to their irrelevance. Now church buildings are regularly converted to apartments and museums or even torn down. The decline of denominational churches happened slowly over many decades. As the fourth beast's secular ideas crept into the Church, they began to look more like the world than the Church. Multiple denominations and other great mentoring organizations such as the Boy Scouts of America succumbed to pressure to yield to the LGBTQ agenda, leading to a perverse decline. Financial trouble ensued, caused by a drop-off in membership or attendance. These attacks required precise planning and battle plans by the fourth beast, yet many Christians failed to recognize the enemy's devices. We need to recognize and ward off these plans in our local church or other character-building organizations.

Become an expert at recognizing infiltration by compromised individuals. Know their strategies: after they are done wrecking a church and attendance drops, they move to the next target. Pastors that fight for the truth and weed out satanic infiltrators attract more church members in the long run, not less.

4. Investments. Many Christians remain ignorant of the investments in their 401k. Paying fees to participate, Christians unwittingly pick mutual funds that invest in companies that support organizations such as Black Lives Matter, Planned Parenthood, LGBTQ initiatives, and the like. If we aren't careful, we will allow the fourth beast to use our own money to advance an evil agenda. I encourage Christians to carefully audit their investments to find out where their money is going. If a company is acting against your values, go to the shareholders' meetings and let management know where you stand. Boycott companies attempting to force-feed satanic values to your family. Collectively, we control enough resources to make a huge difference.

5. Inflation. We are told inflation is normal – two percent or more erosion per year of our buying power is just the way it is. Inflation robs the middle class and enriches the banks, the core control mechanism of the fourth beast system. When the United States operated without a private central bank and instead printed its currency in the mid-1800s, the value of the dollar went up for nearly fifty years. Following the passage of the Federal Reserve Act of 1913, after which a private central bank began to print our money, the dollar declined 98 percent in value over the next one hundred years. This system by design robs wealth from the working class while enriching the banks. With near global private central bank control, the purchasing power of all currencies steadily declined over the last hundred years, making it difficult for people to get ahead – constituting another example of wearing out the saints. Christians can fight back against inflation by investing in real assets like commodities, precious metals, and real estate.

6. Debt. Proverbs 22:7 (AMPC) states, "The rich rule over the poor, and the borrower is servant to the lender." Borrowing puts a person or business under the control of the lender and becomes a form of bondage and debt slavery. Borrowing to pay for a house, car, furniture, and the like, or making purchases on credit, became generally acceptable in our culture. However, saints should realize debt slavery is not God's best plan for any of us. We need to trust God to get out of debt and pay cash for things we want and need. As a graduate of a reputable US-based business school, I discovered the standardized teaching that debt is required for efficient management – debt-free businesses purportedly are mismanaged. Over the years I met scores of entrepreneurs who got into trouble with debt. Debt is attractive because it reduces up-front equity needs, and everything works great when markets are on an upswing. However, companies holding debt often end up getting wiped out by downturns. Since the same groups lending the money also control the finance system and can initiate downturns in the markets, it's only a matter of time before they own great businesses bought in foreclosure situations. Before I received the insight contained in this book, God directed me to get free from debt completely. I believe we need to be free from debt slavery to be able to receive God's full blessing.

When believers trust God, He will show us how to get out of and stay out of debt. Too many of God's people are loaded with debt. As a result, believers work a good portion of their lives just to pay the interest on debt. Debt, a form of slavery, should be avoided altogether.

7. Poison in food, cosmetics, and medicine. In the last chapter, I mention cancer deaths skyrocketed beginning in the twentieth century. I believe cancer is caused in large part by new environmental factors, processed foods, exposure to metals and plastics, and chemicals. Today we are exposed to carcinogenic chemicals in cosmetics, soft drinks, and grain products. Fast foods often are laced with artificial flavors that give them great flavor but lack food value. Lab grown and GMO meats are unproven and could be causing long-term damage. Many fruits and vegetables are covered in harmful pesticides, causing fertility issues as well as contributing to cancer rates. Farm-grown fish often contains high levels of heavy metals and other toxins. As a general anecdotal observation, I find the more woke a food manufacturing corporation is, the more likely the food is contaminated. U.S. water supplies often contain fluoride, known to diminish fertility and lower IQ.[67] Christians keep their immune systems strong by taking control of the food they consume and focusing on organic or locally produced, high-quality food. Invest in a high-quality water filter for your home to remove fluoride, chlorine, and other chemicals. Invest in your health by regularly obtaining laboratory tests for your family to monitor metals, metabolic levels, vitamin deficiencies, and iodine levels.

Many medicines are synthetic petroleum products. The accepted purity in the pharmaceutical industry is 97.5 percent, meaning 2.5 percent of the drug could be contaminated. Try to limit the use of pharmaceutical drugs and research herbal alternatives and homeopathic remedies for common ailments. For instance, there are great herbal alternatives to a common chronic medication for high cholesterol, statins. Berberine is proven to lower cholesterol naturally.[68]

---

[67] Satabdi Saha, "How Can Fluoride Impact Fertility?" *HealthNews*, March 14, 2023, https://healthnews.com/family-health/reproductive-health/how-can-fluoride-impact-fertility/#:~:text=High%20fluoride%20exposure%20is%20linked,reduces%20the%20fertility%20of%20men

[68] Jennifer Moll, "Can Berberine Lower Your Lipid Levels?" *VeryWell Health*, updated July 21, 2021, https://www.verywellhealth.com/berberine-lowers-cholesterol-698106.

8. Indoctrination of children in public schools. I received a quality education in a public grade school. Parents remained involved with the school and let the teachers know when they did not agree with the curriculum. Unfortunately, the public-school system declined considerably since many of us went through the system. Today, many public schools introduce children to complex topics far before they are able to process them, such as gender identity. Confusing topics such as racism are discussed in a divisive way. Many public-school libraries make pornography available to children. Christian parents must get involved on school boards or even take their children out of the public schools and enroll them in private Christian schools or homeschool them. At a minimum, read everything your child reads and talk them through it.

A while ago I met a Hillsdale College professor, Matthew Mehan, who helped a foundation which synthesizes extensive research on the success factors for children that are raised Christian and stay true to their faith through early adulthood. He said a single factor mattered the most: they had parents who would "talk to the TV." He said kids maintain their Christian faith when they have parents who consistently stop a movie or TV show and explain to them how a commercial or other message is seeking to change the way they think. If parents are silent and let the world indoctrinate their children, their children often lose their way. Armed with a new way of thinking, I began to explain to my children the Biblical truths of courtship and marriage and the proper way to treat others. I also began to point out subliminal messages on TV. Overnight, I felt a closer bond to my oldest child. More importantly, I am preparing my children for the secular onslaught that seeks to defile their pure and tender hearts. Our children are our future, and proper training is critical for them to survive the onslaught of satanic messaging.

The fourth beast carefully crafted numerous methods to wear out the saints without our knowledge or consent. Cunning methods moved to the mainstream to the point where we no longer question them. The descriptions provide only a small fraction of the numerous ways the fourth beast methodically wears out the saints. While it might seem overwhelming to process, don't lose sight of the bigger picture. The fourth beast soon dies, and all funding and control mechanisms break down. Soon we all are freed from the fourth beast's tentacles. God calls us to play a part. Will you answer the call?

"The fourth beast is cornered and making mistakes. It's just a matter of time before he dies. Soldier Saints need not fear, but rather boldly seek God concerning their role in the coming Kingdom Age of the Saints."

– Benjamin Thomas

6. The Death of the Fourth Beast

But the judgment shall be set [by the court of the Most High], and they shall take away his dominion to consume it [gradually] and to destroy it [suddenly] in the end.
— Dan. 7:26 AMPC

Announced thousands of years ago, amazing developments redefine our future. The fourth beast dies a brutal and painful death. Satan again fails to achieve his goal of a one-world government and religion. I believe we will witness the death of the seemingly invincible fourth beast in our lifetime:

> I looked then because of the sound of the great words which the horn was speaking. I watched until *the beast was slain and its body destroyed and given over to be burned with fire.* And as for the rest of the beasts, their power of dominion was taken away, yet their lives were prolonged [for the duration of their lives was fixed] for a season and time (Dan. 7:11 AMPC, emphasis added).

We are living at the tail end of the age of the fourth beast. The books of Daniel and Revelation prophesied the fourth beast's destructive and demonic world system causes more destruction than any prior beast and succeeds in wearing out the saints. As described in prior chapters, prophecies concerning the fourth beast are now fulfilled. The fourth beast succeeded in subduing three of the most influential nations on earth to carry out his demonic rule through a manipulative little horn. He convinced the rest of the earth to remain complicit as he wiped out 25 percent or more of humanity. Now the fourth beast comes up squarely with the wrath of God. What causes a system so powerful and well-orchestrated to fall apart? Who kills the fourth beast and how? What is our role? How do Soldier Saints prepare for this epic event?

Slow Decline, then Sudden Death

According to Daniel 7:26, the fourth beast's dominion declines gradually before sudden death. The demise of the fourth beast begins with the judgment seat in heaven. The fourth beast is judged by the Ancient of Days (God) in the court of heaven, and events begin to work against the fourth beast. I am reminded of the Scripture in Revelation showing us how the Father stores the prayers of the saints in vessels. Tangible events happen in the natural when heavenly vases overflow with prayers of the saints. The heavenly vases are brimming with the prayers of the saints. More intercessors pray today than at any time in human history – massive worldwide prayer climaxed in 2020.[69] Judgment falls on the fourth beast when the level of evil and tyranny reaches the point where all civilization is threatened. Daniel 7:21-22 says the "horn made war with the saints and prevailed over them. Until the Ancient of Days came, and judgment was given to the saints of the Most High [God]." The fourth beast wears out the saints, makes war with the saints, and prevails against (or defeats) them, then judgment falls on the fourth beast. Until now, the saints are defeated in the geopolitical dominion of the world and are not witnessing the judgment of the fourth beast, based on natural observation.

    Many think of war as a battlefield where opposing forces draw weapons and charge. Given the complex nature of the fourth beast system, we battle for geopolitical dominion. Christians quietly and steadily proselytize followers worldwide but don't dominate areas such as media, banking, communications, business, education, or government. As Jesus demonstrated, we possess and exercise dominion in the spiritual realm over Satan. However, Satan exercises geopolitical dominion over the world and the saints. As foretold in Scripture, the dominion of the geopolitical and financial realm of the fourth beast is the reason why for two millennia, since the coming of Christ, true Christians failed to dominate the geopolitical

---

69 Jordan Kelly-Linden, "Pandemic Prompts Surge in Interest in Prayer, Google Data Shows," *Telegraph*, May 22, 2020, www.telegraph.co.uk/global-health/climate-and-people/panemic-prompts-surge-interest-prayer-google-data-show.

realm. A former business partner of mine used to say the golden rule means, "he with the most gold rules" – a true statement concerning geopolitical control. The fourth beast controls the wealth and resources to maintain geopolitical dominion and has the cunning to maintain it.

Daniel 7:26 outlines a period of decline of dominion for the fourth beast followed by a sudden decline. The final judgment of the fourth beast happens in a single day. We don't slowly claw our way to rule the world over time, as postmillennialists believe. The Bible clearly articulates the fourth beast possesses the power to wear out the saints until his death. Instead, the grand finale of the stone judgment is a single day takedown of the fourth beast system. In chapter eight I highlight the numerous times in the Bible when God took out impenetrable forces in a single day. Bringing down evil empires in a single day is God's method, for then only He gets the glory. According to Scripture, God plans to eliminate the fourth beast quite suddenly at the end of the age of the fourth beast, in a single day, ending the times of the Gentiles.

Society Waking Up: The Beginning of the End for the Fourth Beast

The acceleration of the decline of the fourth beast starts when humanity, especially Christians, wake up to the fourth beast system and reject it. The fourth beast relies on deception and cover to retain power. The singularly important public wake-up call to how the fourth beast system operates in lockstep with governments and corporations occurred during the Covid pandemic.

The pandemic hit the world newswires in February 2019. Shortly thereafter, governments worldwide implemented synchronous lockdowns of citizens, giving them instruction to stay home if feeling symptoms of Covid similar to the flu. Restricting freedom of movement, governments introduced the idea of essential businesses to the world. Worldwide, pastors began to fight local governments for permission to meet in person with their congregations. Thousands of churches and small businesses closed, never to reopen. Florida district attorney Andrew Warren ordered the arrest of Pastor Rodney Howard-Browne for continuing to conduct church meetings during the Covid-restriction period. I spoke to Rodney Howard-Browne after his release; for several months after his arrest Rodney received calls from pastors worldwide experiencing unprecedented pressure to keep their doors closed under threat of arrest. The power and orchestration of central bodies such as the World Health Organization and the Centers for Disease Control and Prevention, became blatantly obvious to many in the general public. The unelected leaders of these organizations exercised outsized power over supposed sovereign governments. Relatively quickly a vaccine formulary appeared, supposedly the cure for the pandemic, and billions of doses were administered worldwide. Now we know the Covid vaccine and testing procedures, patented years earlier, involved prior planning.[70] Numerous studies show the danger of the shot – injections may lead to severe heart conditions and weakened immunity.[71] The Food and Drug

---

70 David Martin, "The Gathering Storm: When Voice of Reason Is Silenced," *Rumble*, accessed June 6, 2023, https://rumble.com/v2ncp8w-dr-david-e.-martin-phd-covid-summit-european-union-parliament-may-2023.html.

71 Jan Jekielek,"Dr. Peter McCullough & Dr. Aseem Malhotra Discuss the Extraordinary Harm Caused By COVID-19 Vaccines," *Epoch Times*, December 19, 2022; Zachary Stieber, "New Study: Repeated COVID-Vaccination Weakens Immune System, *YourNews.com*, June 5, 2023, https://yournews.com/2023/06/05/2582266/new-study-repeated-covid-19-vaccination-weakens-immune-system.

Administration and other institutions created to protect the public proved complicit beneficiaries of the pandemic.[72]

Ed Dowd, a former BlackRock portfolio manager, analyzed the Covid vaccine from a simple and elegant perspective, excess deaths by year. An excerpt from his book, *"Cause Unknown": The Epidemic of Sudden Deaths in 2021 and 2022*, contains the following:

> By 2017, around 2.8 million Americans died. 2018 was about the same again. 2019, about the same again. Not surprisingly, 2020 saw a spike, smaller than you might imagine, some of which could be attributed to COVID and to the initial treatment strategies that were not effective. But then in 2021, the stats people expected went off the rails. The CEO of OneAmerica insurance company publicly disclosed that during the third and fourth quarters of 2021, death in people of working age (18-64) was 40% higher than it was before the pandemic. Significantly, the majority of the deaths were not attributed to COVID. A 40% increase in deaths is literally earth-shaking, and not only for the devastated families and communities that experience the deaths. Even a 10% increase in excess deaths would have been a 1-in-200-year event. But this was 40%.[73]

In his book Mr. Dowd points out that the only change causing excess deaths was the vaccine itself. Ed wasn't the only one to take notice – society woke up to the tyranny.

---

[72] Aaron Kheriaty, MD, *The New Abnormal: The Rise of the Biomedical Security State* (Washington DC: Regnery, 2022), 125.
[73] Ed Dowd, *"Cause Unknown": The Epidemic of Sudden Deaths in 2021 and 2022* (New York: Skyhorse, 2022), introduction.

Simultaneous with the Covid pandemic, communications from the World Economic Forum centered on a Great Reset, a dystopian society where citizens would own nothing and be happy. Big tech sprang into action and began deplatforming tens of thousands of critics of the Great Reset. The social media platforms scrubbed critics of the Covid vaccine or proponents of alternative treatments such as Ivermectin, by deplatforming them. Censorship became a public issue. The media deplatformed sitting president Donald Trump on Twitter and other platforms. Parler and other alternative platforms designed to compete with Twitter and Facebook launched, but soon these platforms lost their servers and other services on Amazon, Apple, Google, and others.[74]

It became increasingly obvious to many of the public a power structure existed possessing enormous coordinative ability which reached into big corporations and governments. The awe-inspiring amount of sheer command-and-control ability shocked the world. The unholy alliance between business and government predated current events and moved beyond the realm of conspiracy theory. Anyone with experience running organizations recognized the sheer coordination required to implement near-simultaneous worldwide lockdowns, combined with concurrent vaccine rollouts worldwide. This, of course, necessitated careful orchestration and planning before the pandemic. Historically, the span of years necessary to design new vaccines typically extends fifteen years or more.[75] In the case of the Covid pandemic, the vaccines appeared in less than

---

74 Brian Fung, "Parler Has Now Been Booted by Amazon, Apple and Google," *CNN*, updated January 11, 2021, https://www.cnn.com/2021/01/09/tech/parler-suspended-apple-app-store/index.html.
75 Natalie Colarossi and Taylor Ardrey, "How Long It Took to Develop 13 Vaccines in History," *Business Insider*, accessed May 8, 2023, https://www.businessinsider.com/how-long-it-took-to-develop-other-vaccines-in-history-2020-7?op=1

a year. Wise citizens recognized the rushed process and waited for additional data to surface before receiving the injections. Sadly, many others face ongoing health issues.

Based on the events over the last few years, the world woke up to the fourth beast system. In Brazil millions hit the streets protesting the supposed win of former president Luiz Inácio Lula da Silva, who at one time faced corruption charges, against the sitting president Jair Bolsonaro. In China tens of thousands or more protested the draconian Communist Party of China, risking their own lives in the process.[76] Similar protests occurred in Canada, Peru, Denmark, Italy, France, Germany, and Iran. Citizens paid attention to years of unfettered immigration in Europe and even in the United States, designed to destroy national sovereignty, leading to rising crime rates.[77] Inflation exploded worldwide, as evidenced by the skyrocketing cost of food, fuel, and other basics, eroding the purchasing power of citizens. A newly released documentary, *Died Suddenly*, highlights the issue of sudden deaths by recipients of the Covid shots, many of whom are young.[78] Despite efforts by the elite media mouthpieces to hide adverse events, the formerly asleep public awakened. The ratings of mainstream news agencies tanked, and citizens flocked to social media platforms like Telegram and Signal to obtain their news elsewhere. This awakening represents a critical step in the death march of the fourth beast. Worldwide,

---

76 Nick Shifrin and Teresa Cebrian Aranda, "Thousands in China Protest Zero-COVID Policy in Largest Demonstration in Decades," *PBS News Hour*, accessed June 9, 2023, https://www.pbs.org/newshour/show/thousands-in-china-protest-zero-covid-policy-in-largest-demonstrations-in-decades

77 "Migrant Crisis: Migration to Europe Explained in Seven Charts," *BBC*, March 4, 2016, https://www.bbc.com/news/world-europe-34131911; Stephen Collinson, "Everyone Can Now Agree – the U.S. Has a Border Crisis," *CNN*, December 16, 2022, https://www.cnn.com/2022/12/16/politics/biden-immigration-crisis-title-42/index.html

78 *Died Suddenly*, dir. Matthew Miller Skow and Nicholas Stumphauzer, pro. Stew Peters, 2022.

we are seeing an incredible awakening, as if citizens are unplugging from the fourth beast matrix.

Learn to Discern the Times

Many Christians confuse the present time with the End Times. Based on traditional teaching, many in the Church believe the Rapture occurs in times of distress to save the Christians from ensuing judgment. Many Christians believe we live in the time of tribulation outlined in Revelation. One author wrote that we are already experiencing the battle of Armageddon. Given the obvious coordination of power by the fourth beast system across the governments of the world, it's understandable why many Christians are confused. When I first began to comprehend the sheer organization, scale, and reach of the fourth beast system, I became confused and fearful. However, a close examination of Scripture reveals we observe mere shadows of things to come. The fourth beast attempts to bring in the End Times early but fails:

> This king [fourth beast regime] will speak evil
>
> of God Most High,
>
> and he will be cruel
>
> to God's chosen ones.
>
> He will try to change God's Law
>
> and the sacred seasons.
>
> And he will be able to do this
>
> for a time, two times,
>
> and half a time (Dan. 7:25 CEV).

The word *seasons* in Daniel 7:25 means the appointed time. The fourth beast attempts to change his appointed time by accelerating time. He's not trying to reverse time, for to go back would constitute a downgrade in capability. The fourth beast operates with more sophistication, organization, and concealment than the first, second, or third beasts. The fourth beast attempts to advance or accelerate world events to achieve total and complete dominion and destruction – the time of the dragon. The dragon is the *fifth* beast that appears as the anti-Christ, who leads during extreme tribulation on the earth. According to Scripture, during the time of the dragon, the following events occur:

1. The anti-Christ appears – many will be deceived (Rev 13:11-15).

2. Most humans receive a mark, without which people cannot buy or sell goods (Rev 13:16).

3. All sea creatures die (Rev 16:3).

4. The water supply is contaminated (Rev 16:4).

5. Fire destroys a third of the earth (Rev 8:7).

6. Hellish creatures torment a large population of the earth, ruled by the angel of the bottomless pit, Apollyon (Rev 9:6, 11).

7. Plagues and genocide kill a third of humankind (Rev 9:18). (Note: this is in addition to the 25 percent destroyed by the fourth beast.)

8. The Jewish temple is restored (Rev 11:1-2).

These signs occur during the time of great tribulation, a brutal time on earth. A small remnant of true descendants of the ancient tribes of Israel, numbering 144,000, refuse to succumb to the dragon (Rev 14:2-4). The Bible mentions that many refusing to take the mark of the beast suffer death as a result. The fourth beast desires to bring in this particular time earlier than God outlined in the Word.

Now is Not the Time to Fear

Because we catch glimpses of this future, Christians experience confusion and panic, falling back into even *more* extreme rapture paralysis. For instance, digital chips integrated with personal health records are injected into people voluntarily in certain parts of Europe, and this appears as a potential mark of the beast, an indelible personal identifier used for trade purposes, spoken of in Revelation 13:16.[79] Private central banks are pushing digital currency, an additional means of control of the population. Recently, we observed Canadian banks turning off the bank accounts of truck drivers and protesters sympathetic to the drivers' cause.

Near complete control exists in communist China, where millions of security cameras track the movement of citizens, assisted by facial recognition technology. Chinese citizens must toe the party line or be locked out of trade and public transport if their social credit score drops. Chinese citizens' conversations are recorded and interpreted through AI and machine learning, using tracking devices and home-monitoring microphones. This technology is a foreshadow of how the dragon will implement full control in the future. Today, we see a trial run by the fourth beast as he attempts

---

[79] Maddy Savage, "Thousands of Swedes are Inserting Microchips Under Their Skin," *NPR*, October 22, 2018, https://www.npr.org/2018/10/22/658808705/thousands-of-swedes-are-inserting-microchips-under-their-skin

to empower the dragon before his time. But the mere observation of shadows of the future does not mean we live in the time of the anti-Christ. Neither are we living in the time of the Great Tribulation. On the contrary, we live in a glorious time – the time of the destruction of the fourth beast before the Kingdom Age of the Saints.

In Daniel 7:25, we are warned the fourth beast attempts to change God's law. The Hebrew word *law* means command or decree. Through the power and influence of the fourth beast system, Satan attempts to change God's decrees and laws. Specifically, Satan tries to change the original supreme law, the law of the harvest. After the great flood destroyed the earth but Noah's family survived, God set forth a supreme law in Genesis 8:22 (ASV): "While the earth remaineth, seedtime and harvest, and cold and heat, and summer and winter, and day and night shall not cease." The law of the harvest essentially dictates that when bad seeds are sown, a bad harvest follows and vice versa. This law applies to all aspects of life, including farming, procreation, and committing good or evil deeds. Galatians 6:7 (Darby) reinforces the power of the law of the harvest; "Be not deceived, God is not mocked; for whatever a man shall sow, that also shall he reap." The fourth beast minions planted evil seeds for many generations. Simultaneously, the fourth beast controls the world governments, allowing it to operate with legal immunity. As a result, the leaders under the fourth beast don't expect judgment. They are wrong.

Justice is Coming

Many frustrated patriots ask, "When will these people pay for their crimes?" Worldwide, crimes against humanity are sanctioned, at a minimum, or even implemented by our governments.[80] In America, citizens showed up to protest the election in 2020, and many subsequently got incarcerated for more than two years in a Washington, DC, jail with no family visitation, poor diet, and an abusive environment.[81] Scores of political prisoners endured solitary confinement, a form of torture – in a "free" country![82] Whether you agree with the J6 protesters or not, free speech and the right to protest is a constitutionally protected activity in the United States, and these are now political prisoners. I can't imagine the conditions for political prisoners in China and other nonfree nations. Worldwide, justice systems appear to ignore the rights of average citizens and instead protect the elites.

Extreme arrogance causes the fourth beast to believe justice fails. Crime with no punishment is a violation of the supreme law of the harvest. Perversion of justice or changing the law provides a false sense of security for the fourth beast. God directly deals with the fourth beast in a manner that sets Satan back potentially hundreds of years or more. God's judgment decimates corrupt governments worldwide and forces the elites into hiding. The fourth beast cannot change the law.

Satan must rely on human technology to implement his system of control. Innovations such as computer networking, advanced microprocessors, AI, machine learning, facial recognition, the Cloud, and so forth are productivity-enhancing tools used in the

---

80 "Crimes Against Humanity," *Wikipedia.org*, accessed June 8, 2023, https://en.wikipedia.org/wiki/Crimes_against_humanity
81 Jaclyn Diaz, "Jan. 6 Detainees Say a D.C. Jail Is So Awful That They'd Like a Transfer to Guantanamo," *NPR*, October 7, 2022, https://www.npr.org/2022/10/07/1127481476/capitol-riot-detainees-request-guantanamo-transfer-dc-jail-conditions
82 Kerry Picket, "Solitary Confinement for Jan. 6 Riot Participants Draws Criticism from Democratic Senators and ACLU," *Washington Examiner*, June 8, 2021, https://www.washingtonexaminer.com/news/aclu-capitol-rioters-in-solitary-confinement

future to control humanity. The reliance on human creativity and ingenuity reveals Satan's deficiency when compared to the Holy Spirit, who speaks to God's people without the need for these types of technologies. Satan, a fallen angel, cannot rival God's power and strength. Satan can't change God's timeline or the law, despite Satan's best efforts. God limited Satan's dominion during the time of the fourth beast to a certain number of years in the Biblical calendar.

The Mysterious Gap Between the Fourth and Fifth Beast

In Revelation 13:11-12 (NLT) a transition occurs between the time of the fourth beast and the fifth beast, the dragon. "Then I saw *another* beast come up out of the earth. He had two horns like those of a lamb, but he spoke with the voice of a dragon. He exercised all the authority of the first beast." When reading Revelation 13, I asked God a simple question, "What happens between the fourth beast's death and the time of the fifth beast, the dragon?" The answer is in the same passage, Revelation 13:9-10 (MSG) sets the stage for a divine judgment. "They've made their bed; now they must lie in it. Anyone marked for prison goes straight to prison; anyone pulling a sword goes down by the sword. Meanwhile, God's holy people passionately and faithfully stand their ground." The verse indicates a powerful role reversal for the fourth beast – *the hunter becomes the hunted*. The fourth beast, who for a couple of thousand years perverted faith, terrorized Christians, and implemented extreme genocide, now sits in the hot seat of judgment. The judgment process of the fourth beast minions takes time – a slow start followed by a fast, single day finish.

When the fourth beast dies, we enter a new age before the fifth beast comes on the scene. The seven seals in Revelation 6 provide incredible clues. In Revelation 6, Jesus opens seven seals one by one. Many existing End Times books and commentaries teach that the seals are all open at the end of time, during and around the Great Tribulation. However, God showed me this is not the case. The seals of the scroll in Revelation 6 are opened one by one, starting at the beginning of the times of the Gentiles, when pagans rule the earth over four consecutive empires.

The Revelation Scroll

Let's review the first four seals again. The first seal of the scroll is opened in Revelation 6:1-2, described as a white horse conquering with a bow. The first seal represents the first beast, the Chaldean-Babylonian Empire. (The white horse of the first seal differs from the white horse Jesus rides when He returns.) The highly satanic Babylonian Empire destroyed Solomon's temple and exiled the Israelite leaders to Babylon. When the second seal is opened, a red horse takes peace from the earth with a great sword (v. 4). The second seal represents the second beast, the Medo-Persian Empire. The Medo-Persian Empire, established under King Cyrus, who decreed the Israelites could rebuild the temple in Jerusalem, remained pagan and did not represent godly leadership. The third seal introduces a black horse with its rider holding a balance (v. 5). This seal represents the Greco-Macedonian Empire, which instituted progressive leadership and democracy, the alphabet, science, and mathematics. The fourth seal in Revelation 6:8 brought a pale horse, named death. This horse represents the current fourth beast system, with ancient Roman roots. The pale horse was "given power to destroy a fourth of the earth by war, famine, disease, and wild beasts" (Rev 6:8 MSG). Now, the fifth seal opens in Revelation 6:9, and the accumulation of the innocent martyrs' blood cries out to God for righteous judgment (I think of the billion aborted children). A pause occurs and the martyrs are given white robes and told to wait longer (vv. 10-11).

The sixth seal is opened, and the earth's nobility and their subjects are judged and hide in caves because of the severe wrath of God. The time of judgment in Revelation 6:12-17 corresponds to Revelation 13:10, Daniel 7:26, and Daniel 2:34-35, the stone judgment. God steps in and judges the leaders of the earth causing them to hide, fearing for their lives. Only God could orchestrate extreme exposure and judgment so marvelous and complete. The Kingdom Age of the Saints occurs during the sixth seal.

The Stone Judgment and Glory That Follows

The prophet Daniel explains the stone judgment in Daniel 2:34-35 (NLT):

> As you watched, a rock was cut from a mountain, but not by human hands. It struck the feet of iron and clay, smashing them to bits. The whole statue was crushed into small pieces of iron, clay, bronze, silver, and gold. Then the wind blew them away without a trace, like chaff on a threshing floor. But the rock that knocked the statue down became a great mountain that covered the whole earth.

The judgment of the fourth beast shows up in Scripture in numerous places, although it's Daniel that mentions the stone. I love this Scripture. First, we get to watch the judgment occur. Second, the stone hits the feet of the statue and the entire statue is crushed, ending the times of the Gentiles. Third, the rock that knocked the statue down then covers the earth. I believe this signifies the coming glory of God that fills the earth. So, the judgment of the fourth beast then ushers in the glory of God.

Staying with the theme of the glory, let's also look at Daniel 7:9-11 (YLT):

> I was seeing till that thrones have been thrown down, and the Ancient of Days is seated, His garment as snow is white, and the hair of his head is as pure wool, His throne flames of **fire**, its wheels burning **fire**. A flood of **fire** is proceeding and coming forth from before Him, a thousand thousands do serve Him, and a myriad of myriads before Him do rise up, the Judge is seated and the books have been opened. I was seeing, then, because of the voice of the great words that the horn is speaking, I was seeing till that the beast is slain, and his body hath been destroyed, and given to the burning **fire** (bold emphasis).

In these three verses, fire is mentioned four times. Three times referring to the elements surrounding God, and once as the consuming fire that burns the fourth beast. I interpret this to mean the judgment of the fourth beast connects to the fire of God. The fire of God judges the fourth beast and his operatives severely. The judgment of the fourth beast is mentioned in numerous scriptural prophecies – without doubt predestined to occur. The extreme level of pent-up wrath by God toward the fourth beast is expressed clearly in Scripture – an epic judgment event comes to the fourth beast. However, the fire and glory of God manifests, stays on the earth and ushers in a global revival for the Church. To the fourth beast, the fire equals destruction. To the Church, the fire manifests the power and presence of God.

The Stone Judgment and Sixth Seal Aren't Explained by Other End Times Theories

The sixth seal represents a critical marker, the end of the fourth beast and end of the times of the Gentiles. The opening of the sixth seal unleashes a time of judgment – the stone judgment. Other End Times theories fail to explain the stone judgment. The seventh seal represents the Great Tribulation, which precedes the battle of Armageddon. The nobles of the earth are judged *before* the seventh seal is opened. The "other" judgment event preceding the battle of Armageddon presents a problem for the great preponderance of End Times theories:

1. A very common viewpoint today is premillennialism. Premillennialists believe Jesus returns prior to the millennium, when He reigns for a thousand years, a time when Satan is locked up. The age of the Church is the time until Jesus comes. Suffering generally increases as history progresses until suddenly Christ returns.[83] While I agree with many tenants of premillennialism, I don't agree that suffering continues until Christ returns. There is no accommodation for the sixth seal or the stone judgment. Moreover, Daniel 7 speaks of a transition of dominion to the saints after the fourth beast

---

83 Matt Shores, "Biblical Prophecy: Four Views of the End Times," *ExploreGod.com*, accessed June 21, 2023, https://www.exploregod.com/articles/biblical-prophecy-four-views-of-the-end-times

dies, which premillennialists neglect to include. In premillennialism, judgment of evil strictly occurs during the battle of Armageddon.

2. Dispensationalism, a type of premillennialism, provides for the additional concept of a rapture event that removes Christians from earth before Jesus returns. Some believe the Rapture happens prior to the Great Tribulation, some believe the Rapture happens in the middle, and others believe that Christians must endure the Great Tribulation. Dispensationalists also believe suffering generally increases as history progresses. Again, there is no accommodation for the sixth seal, the stone judgment of the evil of the earth prior to the Great Tribulation. While I agree with the dispensationalists that a rapture occurs, I believe it occurs while the saints are ruling and after the full glory of God covers the earth.

3. Postmillennialism maintains that Jesus will return after the millennium, and the Church leads in a progressively more positive environment, as the gospel is spread. The millennium is gradually and progressively established on earth when universal peace reigns on earth as a result of the work of the Church spreading the gospel. The issue here is threefold. First, postmillennialism fails to accommodate the judgment event for the evil nobles of the earth, the sixth seal, synonymous with the stone judgment. The second issue is,

according to Daniel 7:26, the judgment of the fourth beast culminates with a sudden ending. The stone judgment deals decisively with the fourth beast rule in an accelerated event. Representing the third issue, until the time of judgment, the fourth beast possesses power to wear out the saints. According to Scripture, until the fourth beast is slain, no amount of preaching the gospel leads to geopolitical control. History proves the point – the fourth beast wore out Christians for over two millennium, a fulfillment of Biblical prophecy.

4. Amillennialism represents another viewpoint, similar to postmillennialism, but they believe that the millennium is a present reality. The millennium is now – it's the Church age, the entire period between the departure and return of Jesus. Amillennialists point out that the only mention of the millennium is in Revelation and thus is subject to interpretation as an indeterminate period of time. Again, this theory neglects the stone judgment, the sixth seal. The theory also overlooks the way that God operated in the past. God warned Abraham that Israel would be in bondage for 430 years and be delivered. He warned Israel, through the prophets, of the coming ages of secular rule, including Babylon, Persia, Greece, and Rome with specific timelines attached. Jesus spoke of the times of the Gentiles during His ministry on earth (Luke 21:24), and pointed out that the times of the Gentiles must be fulfilled. Also, just

look around today, Christians fail to dominate the seven pillars of society.

5. Preterists argue that all the prophecies and occurrences in the Bible that most people think are future events actually happened already – that Christ has already returned. The year AD 70 is central to preterism, the year they argue that Jesus returned. Preterists believe that judgment of evil is a process being fulfilled. This theory suffers the same issues as amillennialism. In addition, by AD 70 the Roman Empire, the root of the fourth beast, did not achieve full control of the nations. The prophet Daniel discussed the fourth beast as a venerable satanic foe to the Church, and history proved Daniel correct. The Roman rule did not end in AD 70.

In Daniel 12:4 (AMPC), God instructs Daniel, "But you, O Daniel, shut up the words and seal the Book until the time of the end. [Then] many shall run to and fro and search anxiously [through the Book], and knowledge [of God's purposes as revealed by His prophets] shall be increased and become great." This Scripture indicates not all prophecies by Daniel are understood until the time of fulfillment. We clearly see what God said about Babylon, Persia, and Greece because of hindsight. Prophecies concerning the fourth beast and little horn are less clear to us *because we live in the age of the fourth beast.* God's plans for humanity are better than we could ask or think. His glorious plan involves judging our oppressors, setting us up to succeed, and releasing His glory in the earth.

The Saints Judge the Fourth Beast

The status of the saints changes when the fourth beast dies. The "they" in Daniel 7:26 (see initial chapter verse) are the saints of God. In Daniel 7:22 (AMPC), the Bible specifically says "judgment was given to the saints of the Most High [God]." We play a role in the death of the fourth beast and in removing his dominion. One year before the 2020 U.S. election, the Lord led me to pray for America and the upcoming election for two hours daily for a year. In addition, I joined in prayer vigils happening worldwide over various online channels. Millions of intercessors globally joined in the prayer fight. Something big happened in the spirit realm – unprecedented intercessory prayer going forth during this time exceeded comprehension, setting world records. A remarkable time of prayer occurred on the mall in Washington, DC, dubbed "the Return," where we collectively repented for the bloodshed of aborted children in America. Forty-two million people watched the livestream and 250,000 people attended from 180 countries.[84] The spiritual fervor remained high as repeated and prayerful marches occurred in Washington, DC, and organized prayer took place around the world. Today, millions of saints are praying for revival. We are starting to see revival break out in some of our universities, such as in Asbury, Kentucky. The revivals in the universities are only a small taste of what is to come.

I will never forget watching President Trump fly off in Air Force One to the tune of Frank Sinatra's "I Did It My Way" at Andrews Air Force Base on January 20, 2021. Many of us shed tears that day. Accusations of election fraud abounded and many good patriots

---

84 "The Return," Washington, DC. September 2020, https://thereturn.org/thereturn-washingtondc.

cried foul. Since the day President Trump left office, I possess an unexplainable inner peace despite grim natural circumstances. Looking back, President Trump's greatest accomplishments included waking up people to the corruption of the media and the system. While the election outcome left questions, the world became permanently more alive and awake to the incestuous nature of the fourth beast system as a result of President Trump's efforts. Trump's inaugural speech in 2017 directly targeted the fourth beast control mechanisms – I encourage you to listen to Trump's initial speech again. President Trump shocked many by pointing to the mainstream news crews at rallies, saying, "See those people; that's fake news." He caused the masses to question the mainstream media for the first time. So many Christians woke up and prayed for the 2020 election. We universally sensed an inflection point – a battle in the spirit world. My time of prayer and reflection unlocked the fresh insight from the Bible I am sharing with you now.

The inner peace I experienced after January 20, 2021, confused me. It appeared on the surface the United States surpassed the point of no return. Corruption appeared to win the day once again. However, as I started my prayer routine for the nation the next day, I felt God say, "You don't need to pray anymore, I have this." Even more confused, I began to dig into the Scriptures to understand what I believed about the End Times and discover a plausible explanation for the peace I felt in my heart. After nearly two years of seeking God in prayer, the Scriptures unlocked truths to me as if scales came off my eyes. Passages that I read many times before came alive. I realized that the Church is on the cusp of a major breakthrough as we enter a new age. Today, prophecies come forth nearly daily through the ministry of Julie Green Ministries and others, promising judgment to the mafia in control of the seven pillars of society. After tuning into prophetic voices for over 20 years, I now see an acceleration of geopolitical prophecies coming forth from many reliable prophetic voices. A major event is brewing in the spirit realm.

Who Kills the Fourth Beast?

The fourth beast implodes, in part, by an internal civil war among the fourth beast power structures. Revelation 17:16-17 (MSG) sets the stage for a civil war within the fourth beast's governance:

> The ten horns you saw, together with the Beast, will turn on the Whore – they'll hate her, violate her, strip her naked, rip her apart with their teeth, then set fire to her. It was God who put the idea in their heads to turn over their rule to the Beast until the words of God are completed. The woman you saw is the great city, tyrannizing the kings of the earth.

As described in chapter four, the whore represents the Vatican, today closely aligned with the Rothschild elites. The same nations that yielded their power and authority to the fourth beast now turn on the little horn and their corrupt elite overlords. The words "rip her apart with their teeth" could be an indication the military participates. However, only God will get the glory for the brutal and deserving end to the rule of the fourth beast.

Are We Witnessing the Final Battle of the Little Horn?

Daniel 11:44-45 (NLT) describes the final battle involving the destruction of the little horn of the fourth beast; "Then news from the east and the north will alarm him [the little horn], and he will set out in great anger to destroy and obliterate many. He will stop between the glorious holy mountain and the sea and will pitch his royal tents. But while he is there, his time will suddenly run out, and no one will help him." In the Bible, directions such as north or south are typically given in relation to Israel (the "glorious holy mountain" mentioned in this verse). The news from the east and north quite possibly refers to the current conflict between Ukraine (north) and Russia (east). Modern-day Ukraine represents the epicenter of the former Khazarian empire. Russia defeated the Khazarians in AD 1000, displacing them from their homeland. The Khazarians then scattered to Western Europe and began infiltrating the world finance system. While the Khazarians possess incredible wealth, they rely on co-opting armies to fight their battles, representing a significant weakness. Over the past two decades, Putin systematically reduced Russia's sovereign debt, never a popular move with the bankers. Russia's special military operation in Ukraine plows on despite massive sanctions inflicted by the United States and Western Europe.

The 2023 World Economic Forum meeting in Davos, Switzerland, omitted Russia for the first time in years. Russia steadily adds new allies in the potential fight against NATO. BlackRock CEO and Chairman Larry Fink admitted that the elites have failed to usher in a New World Order following President Putin's invasion of Ukraine.[85] Only time will tell whether the Russia-Ukraine conflict spells the end for the little horn, the leader of the fourth beast. However, the Bible indicates when the end comes for the little horn, no one will help him.

---

85 "BlackRock Head Admits: "Our New World Order Has Failed"", *Planet Today*, Accessed August 14, 2023. https://www.planet-today.com/2022/03/blackrock-head-admits-our-new-world.html

The end of the rule of the little horn causes the fourth beast to scatter in disarray. Bribes and blackmail hold the fourth beast system together. When the money dries up and crimes are exposed, it won't take long to fall apart. Will you lead the fight to end it?

7. Dominion Transfer to the Saints

Good people leave their wealth to their grandchildren, but a sinner's wealth is stored up for good people.
– Prov 13:22 NCV

When the fourth beast dies, dominion over the earth transfers to the saints, ushering in a divine era of peace and prosperity. The exposure of the inner workings of the fourth beast horrifies the average citizen, and unlikely alliances emerge. The stone judgment prophesied in Daniel 2:35 literally wipes the fourth beast off the map. An unprecedented time of prosperity for the saints ensues, similar to the mighty deliverance Israel experienced after God delivered them from many generations of slavery under Egypt. God calls a new breed of Soldier Saints to rebuild the world. Are you one of the Soldier Saints called to lead in the new age? If you made it this far in the book, I believe you are.

Soldier Saints can sense divine opportunity in the decline of the fourth beast. The system that held us in slavery for over two millennia falls apart, and we stand up and lead a new system. Does this mean everything becomes a bed of ease for the saints? No – our workload amplifies. Get ready to work harder than any time in your whole life. You see, we are called to be salt and light to the world. When the world system falls apart, we are called to help people find their way. The Church replaces governments as the welfare system and also the leadership of the world. Get ready to put your hand to the plow. Money no longer remains an obstacle – managing your time efficiently requires a special anointing and prayerful meditation each and every day.

Fourth Beast Merchants – Major Corporations

The death of the fourth beast devastates power brokers who benefited from corrupt commerce in the fourth beast system. In Revelation 18 we are provided a rich description of the judgment of the fourth beast. Verse 11 (ASV) says "The merchants of the earth weep and mourn over her, for no man buyeth their merchandise any more." In verse 12 it goes on to describe every manner of merchandise, including gold (i.e., currency), wine, jewelry, luxury clothing, and so on. Verse 13 ends by mentioning the same merchants' trade in human souls. Trading in souls includes slave labor and human trafficking. Today, slavery and human trafficking are rampant worldwide. As the atrocious practices of the fourth beast system are exposed, people stop buying from the corporations aligned with the fourth beast, causing a massive wave of insolvency. Righteous judges and military forces seize many businesses and assets aligned with the fourth beast. The shutting down of commerce with fourth beast merchants already started. For instance, the Walt Disney Company lost nearly half its market value in 2022, following their decision to fully embrace the radical LGBTQ activism and declare war on Florida by opposing the state's Parental Rights in Education Act. While Disney's trend from wholesome family entertainment to dark and demoralizing content persisted over several decades, the recent exposure woke up consumers on a broad scale. Recently, both Anheuser-Busch and Target lost significant value after publicly embracing the extreme LGBTQ agenda. The trend of boycotting corrupt businesses will continue, as the unholy alliance between major corporations and the fourth beast is exposed.

The Satanic Depopulation Agenda

Revelation 18:23-24 provides additional insight into the future, "for thy merchants were the princes of the earth; for with thy sorcery were all the nations deceived. And in her was found the blood of prophets and of saints, and of all that have been slain upon the earth." The many corporations aligned with the fourth beast system are held accountable for participating in the tyranny of the fourth beast while also profiting from it. The stated vision of the fourth beast elite is to depopulate the planet. The Georgia Guidestones, erected in 1980 in northeastern Georgia, clearly articulated the goals of the elite. The expensive nineteen-foot-tall rock monument supported a twelve-ton capstone. Designers of the monument etched the first guide: to "Maintain humanity under 500,000,000 in perpetual balance with nature," and translated the words into eight different languages. Many hold Ted Turner, the founder of CNN, responsible for funding the Georgia Guidestones, which were blown up in July 2022.[86] In 1996 Turner famously told *Audubon* magazine that "A total population of 250-300 million people, a 95 percent decline from present levels, would be ideal." He later donated $1 billion to the United Nations. While the funding of the Georgia Guidestones monument remains a mystery, the messaging is eerily similar to language coming out of the United Nations Biodiversity Treaty and the Club of Rome. In a 2010 TED Talk, "Innovating to Zero," Bill Gates said, "With better health care and improved access to vaccines, the world's population could reduce by 10 percent to 15 percent."[87] Henry Kissinger, an adviser to numerous U.S. presidents, stated, "Depopulation should be the highest priority of foreign policy towards the third world, because the U.S. economy will require large and increasing amounts of minerals from abroad, especially from less developed countries."[88] The demonic concept of depopulating humanity guides the elites' agenda.

Fourth Beast Collusion in Action

The Covid pandemic demonstrated the wicked concept of profiting from the depopulation agenda. Governments used the people's tax dollars to enrich the shareholders of the vaccine manufacturers, who manufactured a substance that increases the risk of death and

---

86 The Georgia Guidestones were blown up on July 7, 2022. See Devon M. Sayers and Jamiel Lynch, "Authorities Are Searching for Whoever Set Off an Explosion at a Mysterious Georgia Monument," *CNN*, updated July 7, 2022, https://www.cnn.com/2022/07/07/us/georgia-guidestones-explosion/index.html.
87 Bill Gates, "Innovating to Zero!," *TED2010*, accessed April 28, 2023, https://www.ted.com/talks/bill_gates_innovating_to_zero.
88 Henry Kissinger, *Quotefancy.com*, accessed April 28, 2023, https://quotefancy.com/quote/1275703/Henry-Kissinger-Depopulation-should-be-the-highest-priority-of-foreign-policy-towards-the

other ailments (see chap. 6). The alignment between government and corporate interests was exposed to the public during the Covid pandemic. Many of the unsuspecting victims of vaccine injuries are Christians. Planned Parenthood serves as another example of depopulation for profit with the abortion agenda. Following the recent Roe v. Wade decision by the U.S. Supreme Court, Planned Parenthood pivoted to gender reassignment procedures, more profitable than abortions and rendering victims permanently sterile. With shocking speed and efficiency, the U.S. public school systems began indoctrinating our children to question their gender, providing a steady pipeline for Planned Parenthood surgical suites.

The Roaches Scatter

As God's judgment of the fourth beast rolls out, the fourth beast merchants distance themselves from their elite handlers. Revelation 18:9-10 (MSG) explains, "The kings of the earth will see the smoke of her burning, and they'll cry and carry on, the kings who went night after night to her brothel. They'll keep their distance for fear they'll get burned." A perverse sexual component exists in the alignment between the kings of the earth and the fourth beast overlords. As we uncover more information, we find many governments complicit in human trafficking and organ harvesting of babies and children.[89] Many at the top echelon of the political system willingly participate in ritualistic and satanic practices. Revelation 18:9 indicates these participants are upset when the game ends and God judges the fourth beast. They enjoy their life of sin and suffer few consequences until judgment comes.

---

[89] Anna Fletcher, "Government Complacency and Complicity in Human Trafficking," *GlobalJusticeBlog.com*, November 25, 2014, https://law.utah.edu/government-complacency-and-complicity-in-human-trafficking.

When the sixth seal opens in Revelation 6, a major shaking and judgment occur:

> I watched while he ripped off the sixth seal; a bone-jarring earthquake, sun turned black as ink, moon all bloody, stars falling out of the sky like figs shaken from a tree in high wind, sky snapped shut like a book, islands and mountains sliding this way and that. And then pandemonium, everyone and his dog running for cover – kings, princes, generals, rich and strong, along with every commoner, slave or free. They hid in mountain caves and rocky dens, calling out to mountains and rocks, "Refuge! Hide us from the One Seated on the Throne and the wrath of the Lamb! The great day of their wrath has come – who can stand it!" (Rev 6:12-17).

The vivid picture of an intense spiritual battle in the heavens, combined with visible signs on the earth, reveals the wrath of God toward the fourth beast and the time of public judgment. The stars falling from the sky may signify satanic principalities in charge of certain regions of the earth falling from their positions. Many elites flee into underground bunkers to hide but are discovered and judged. Governments worldwide set up bunkers for doomsday and nuclear war situations, and elites seek refuge in bunkers built using taxpayer money.[90] When the judgment of God begins, an internal civil war erupts within the ten horns, involving the militaries of the world. Military powers recognize humanity ends if the fourth beast achieves its ultimate objective, the depopulation of the earth.

---

[90] Christopher Klein, "Inside the Government's Top-Secret Cold War Hideouts," *History.com*, updated August 23, 2018, https://www.history.com/news/inside-the-governments-top-secret-doomsday-hideouts

Satan hates humanity to such a degree he would like nothing more than to wipe out God's creation. Satan pushes military leaders to issue orders exceeding their collective conscience, and they revolt. Extreme genocidal orders ultimately backfire and the elites are snuffed out, ending the tyranny of the fourth beast rule for a season.

Revelation 6 also indicates the sky closes or snaps shut. On numerous occasions the fourth beast attempted to use technology to open portals into the spiritual realm and release the dragon, the *fifth* beast, before his time. In 2016 the *Wall Street Journal* published an article titled "CERN is Seeking Secrets of the Universe, or Maybe Opening the Portal of Hell."[91] Based in Switzerland, CERN is home to a Large Hadron Collider (LHC), a seventeen-mile subterranean loop on the France-Switzerland border near Geneva that smashes particles at nearly the speed of light. CERN scientists' efforts to investigate extra dimensions and a parallel universe through the LHC are a direct attempt to bring in the dragon, who, according to the book of Revelation, ascends from the bottomless pit into our natural world. During test runs of the LHC, photographers observed strange cloud-and-lightning formations above CERN. Satanic dances and rituals accompanied the test runs at CERN.[92] Efforts to open portals cease and any open portals close when the sixth seal opens in Revelation 6. The fourth beast's judgment and death are complete – all accomplices are judged in the process.

---

91 John Letzing, "CERN Is Seeking Secrets of the Universe, or Maybe Opening the Portals of Hell," *Wall Street Journal*, April 4, 2016, https://www.wsj.com/articles/cern-is-seeking-secrets-of-the-universe-or-maybe-opening-the-portals-of-hell-1459800113

92 Elizabeth Daoud, "A Video Shows Researchers in Switzerland Performing a Satanic Sacrifice as a Macabre Joke," News.com, August 19, 2016, https://www.news.com.au/technology/a-video-shows-researchers-in-switzerland-performing-a-satanic-sacrifice-as-a-macabre-joke/news-story/1cb0e0ab74036d25e5988ea46e8c1eff

Dominion Transfer

The first four beasts in Daniel 7 exercise geopolitical rule over the earth. The word *dominion* refers to governmental dominion or rule. Dominion includes all seven pillars of society, which include religion, family, education, business, government, media, and arts. The dominion each of the four beasts enjoy lasts a limited time. Scholars marvel at the predictive accuracy of Daniel in describing the sequence of power shifts between the four beast systems and how every detail matched later events with remarkable accuracy. The Bible remains the only book that foretells the future in this way – God faithfully shows His people His plans. After the fourth beast is slain, a miracle happens. The dominion in the geopolitical realm is transferred to the saints of God: "I beheld, and the same horn [the fourth beast] made war with the saints, and prevailed against them, until the ancient of days came, and judgment was given to the saints of the Most High, and *the time came that the saints possessed the kingdom* [or reign]" (Dan. 7:21-22 ASV, emphasis added).

The word *possessed* means "to rule" or "to take over." The word *kingdom* translates as "reign" or "sovereignty." The saints will rule over the seven pillars of society. Today, God preserves and prepares a remnant of His servants to lead the seven pillars of society. Governments will shrink to a fraction of the current size, serving a minuscule role as a public service or a utility. Small media outlets owned by people of integrity, faithfully sharing the truth, suddenly blossom and flourish after years of struggle. Technologies long ago discovered to benefit humanity but suppressed by the elite will be released to the public. Saints will pick up pieces of now-defunct corporations at a discount and build new companies selling quality products using godly leadership principals. The finance world will radically change: private central banks will be eliminated and replaced with frictionless and seamless trading mechanisms, using blockchain exchanges. Health cures from plants and nature are rediscovered along with new healing technology, rending current hospital systems and pharmaceuticals obsolete. Poisons are removed from our food, water, and environment, causing cancers to radically diminish. Society celebrates and reinforces the nuclear family, and the gay community produces the most powerful Christian evangelists ever to walk the earth. Children are educated on the classical arts and the world's true history and are taught to walk as mighty men and women of God. The wealth stolen and hoarded by the fourth beast is returned to the people, eliminating hunger and poverty. The glory of God will fill the earth, and revival will break out worldwide.

Soldier Saints

The saints will judge the agents of the fourth beast following the defeat of the head, the little horn. I believe the judging process will be brief. However, the Bible also refers to kings as judges. The saints secure a pivotal role in judging the land during the Kingdom Age of the Saints as kings. Saints are put in charge of the world in a geopolitical sense, armed with a greater understanding of the power of the spirit world established by Jesus when He gave the Church its Great Commission and taught His followers to take authority over Satan. The hundreds of years Satan worked to organize the world into the New World Order leads to failure. The elites not executed or imprisoned after Nuremberg-style trials will go into hiding and die. During the saints' age, God's glory tangibly visits and fills the earth. God did not show me (yet) how long the saints rule the earth, but I sense it lasts hundreds of years. This is the time for the saints to rule in righteousness during a glorious age. This time is profoundly important for the work of the kingdom.

The dominion transfer represents a complete work. Even the remnants of the dominion of the first three beasts are taken away for a season. "As for the rest of the beasts, their dominion was taken away: yet their lives were prolonged for a season and time" (Dan. 7:12). Combining the revelation of Daniel 7 with the insight of Revelation 13, I believe the fourth beast rulers are judged by God and His people, the evil princes of the earth go into hiding, and the saints of God rule the earth during this time both spiritually *and* geopolitically. Soldier Saints judge the fourth beast in physical battle. They will heed the command in Revelation 18:6 (NLT), to:

> Do to her as she has done to others.
>
> > Double her penalty for all her evil deeds.
>
> She brewed a cup of terror for others,
>
> > so brew twice as much for her.

Soldier Saints include military leaders and troops who are not on board with the fourth beast plans to destroy humanity. They will seek out the elites in hiding and eliminate them or otherwise bring them to justice. The elite built mighty fortresses to protect themselves – rooting them out involves great bloodshed. Other Soldier Saints include honorable politicians, judges, attorneys, and others tasked with gathering evidence against the fourth beast rulers to bring them to justice.

Removing Idols – A Commandment

Once Soldier Saints remove evil leaders from our midst, we must execute another step to heal our land. God calls Soldier Saints to remove the idols from our midst. Listen to the commandment God gave to Israel in Deuteronomy 12:2-3 (CEV):

> But the nations that live there worship other gods. So after you capture the land, you must completely destroy their places of worship – on mountains and hills or in the shade of large trees. Wherever these nations worship their gods, you must tear down their altars, break their sacred stones, burn the sacred poles used in worshiping the goddess Asherah, and smash their idols to pieces. Destroy these places of worship so completely that no one will remember they were ever there.

At the time, the Canaanites installed Asherah poles all over the land to signify their worship of the god of fertility. According to ancient mythology, Asherah was the wife of El, who mothered 70 gods, including Baal.[93] Asherah worship involved child sacrifice, especially the firstborn child of the person making a sacrifice. God called on Israel to thoroughly purge the pagan gods.

Any inanimate object worshiped as a god by man instead of God carries a curse. On January 21, 2022, the city of New Orleans replaced the statue of General Lee, a military hero who historians believe singlehandedly defeated the Mexicans in the Mexican-American War, with a lewd statue of Mami Wata. Mami Wata represents a pagan goddess worshiped in West Africa and

---

[93] Mary Fairchild, "Who Is Asherah in the Bible", *Learn Religions*, November 28, 2022, https://www.learnreligions.com/asherah-in-the-bible-6824125.

the Caribbean.[94] As mentioned, atop the U.S. Capitol building sits a statue of the Roman goddess Persephone, ruler of the dead. Recently, New York city installed a goat-like "Baphomet" statue, used by The Satanic Temple, on a New York City courthouse. Soldier Saints need to remove these idols to cleanse our land. However, we should not stop there. There are literally thousands of pagan "gods" among us that warrant removal, including in the establishment Christian churches. There are numerous resources available on pagan symbolism readers should study. If you are like me, you will be shocked and horrified at how paganism surrounds us, especially regarding pedophilia – a heinous crime.

Finally, when Soldier Saints remove the idols, we are to utterly destroy them. In Deuteronomy 13:16, God commands Israel to burn the idols in the public square. We are not to store them in museums or in our homes. We need to destroy them forever to rid our land of the curse.

He Who Possesses the Gold Rules

When God delivered the children of Israel from bondage in Egypt, a transfer of wealth occurred. The Egyptians loaded the departing chosen people with their gold, jewelry, livestock, and apparel. During the transition to the Kingdom Age of the Saints, a transfer of wealth occurs unlike anything the world has ever seen. For centuries the godless elite hoarded the vast majority of the world's resources into large asset pools. In the kingdom age the asset pools are distributed to enlightened stewards, trained in the gift of giving. Hunger and poverty disappear as abundance pours over the earth. We lived under fourth beast slavery for so many generations, it may take a

---

[94] "Mami Wata", *Wikipedia.org*, Accessed July 25,2023. https://en.wikipedia.org/wiki/Mami_Wata

while for people to break out of the slavery mentality. Saints looking for wealth transfer and trained in stewardship are early recipients of the wealth transfer. In the Kingdom Age of the Saints, humanity is freed from debt and subsistence slavery, and many are drawn to God as a result. The saints will work hard, gathering the harvest.

Glory to God! This is great news for the saints on the earth. This revelation is one of hope and excitement. I believe we, the saints of God, are living in the most significant time since Jesus walked the earth. This is the most thrilling time to be alive; we are the generation to witness the brutal takedown of the fourth beast and watch the satanic leaders retreat for a long, long time.

Revival is Coming

The incredible coming revival amounts to much more than fiery preaching. God's glory will fall powerfully – men and women will come to know God in their cars and workplaces. Humanity will marvel at the goodness of God when the fourth beast's assets are redistributed and humanitarian projects are prioritized. When the shroud of deception, brainwashing, and control lifts off the world, there will be a lot of work to do. For centuries societies existed under the rule of the fourth beast, and the saints will function as light bearers to explain where we are in God's timeline and minister the gospel to the people. I believe God will raise up godly leaders who are led by the Holy Spirit to rule with justice as we face this new chapter in humanity.

God's glory will fall in unlikely places spontaneously, such as Kanye Wests' Sunday Service and in public squares. Many initially attracted to God's glory-filled services are riddled with tattoos, coming out of a life of crime, sexual deviance, or drugs – they know they need God. The big question is which churches will embrace the glory of God – many won't. God knocked on the door of many of the established institutions for many years, but they rejected the move of the Holy Spirit. Remember, Jesus sparked revival using an unlikely band of fisherman and other outcasts, confusing the church leaders of the day. The next glory revolution likely mimics the first. Soldier Saints, knowing what comes next, immediately recognize the glory, and run to it – we don't need the blessing of establishment leaders. When we experience God's tangible presence, we want more. Church leaders who move aside and let the Holy Spirit work will see their congregations swell with those hungry for God. Those who don't shrink into oblivion and the sea of forgetfulness.

Hidden for centuries, the revelation of the death of the fourth beast and the transfer of dominion to the saints should invigorate our faith and hope. After reading the Bible many times, I missed this good news until now, as did most. I accepted the common rescue rapture theology when I read Revelation, Daniel, Isaiah, and other prophetic books. Only after crying out to God for many months did I begin to gain new insight and make divine connections in the wonderful Word of God. This caused me to jump out of my chair in excitement.

Soldier Saints will study God's Word regarding the Kingdom Age of the Saints and make an adjustment inside their hearts and minds to raise their level of expectation for the future. We don't want to miss out on the awesome plans God outlined for our future. Rapture during a time of duress became a church doctrine that we need to shed. In the Bible, God never runs from Satan. Sure, sin and idolatry caused God's people to live under the curse at many points in human history. However, as God's people cried out, He always raised up prophets to declare a time of victory and subsequently raised up Soldier Saints to lead God's people out of the dark place and into a place of peace and fellowship with God. The Old Testament provides numerous examples of God responding to the prayers of His people by eliminating evil governments or sieges. God loves to perform these miracles in a single day event where only He gets the glory. In the next chapter, we cover a few of the stories of divine redemption. Meditate on these accounts from the Bible over and over – allow them to sink in and stir up hope for the future. God never changes – if God did it before, He will do it again. Choosing to believe God is up to you.

"The account of the supernatural deliverance of Israel from Egypt in the book of Exodus represents a type and shadow of the ending of the times of the Gentiles. Israel recovered their health, their wealth, and their freedom in divine reparations. I believe the coming deliverance from the slavery of the fourth beast system, which wore out the saints for over two millennia, will set Satan back hundreds of years or more."

– Benjamin Thomas

8. Treasure in Fallen Fortresses

He brought [Israel] forth with silver and gold, and there was not one feeble person among their tribes. Egypt was glad when they departed, for the fear of them had fallen upon the people.
– Ps. 105:37-38 AMPC

Humanity has endured under the rule of fourth beast system for over two millennia and counting. The fourth beast continuously wears out the saints using a variety of methods. Pervasive worldwide, the fourth beast – the finance and governance system – seems unstoppable. Right now it appears that deep state forces in charge of the system are blocking justice. There is nothing new under the sun – the same tyranny occurred in Biblical times. The Bible provides several examples where God's people receive supernatural deliverance under similar circumstances. When impenetrable fortresses come down, God gets the glory. Impenetrable fortresses in the Bible were typically removed in a single day and accompanied by a corresponding wealth transfer. The greatest example of this is in the book of Exodus when Israel was delivered from over four hundred years of slavery.

Israel in Egypt

Egypt built a formidable kingdom before the arrival of Joseph, son of Jacob. However, the turn of events that followed Joseph's arrival in Egypt was incredible. Joseph was the younger of many sons of Jacob and the grandson of Abraham. Jacob's favoritism toward Joseph enraged his brothers, so they sold Joseph into slavery and lied to Jacob, telling him a wild animal killed Joseph. Yet Joseph quietly flourished in Egypt even with slave status – men quickly recognized Joseph's leadership skills and put him in charge of their estates. Even Egypt's head jailer put Joseph, now a convict, in charge of the other prisoners.

The anointing of Joseph's life extended beyond leadership, for God also gave Joseph the ability to interpret dreams. Joseph interpreted a dream (or nightmare) for Pharaoh that changed the course of humanity. In the dream God showed Pharaoh that seven years of plenty would be succeeded by seven years of extreme famine, and Egypt needed to prepare. Pharaoh listened to Joseph, and because Egypt stocked up during times of plenty, Egypt flourished in times of lack. Genesis 41:57 (AMPC) states, "All countries came to Egypt to Joseph to buy grain, because the famine was severe over all [the known] earth." Through Joseph's wisdom, Egypt essentially cornered the food market and forced all nations to trade with Egypt to stay alive. Pharaoh became an extremely wealthy ruler, collecting gold and silver from other nations in exchange for food. At this stage Egypt likely had huge silver and gold deposits from their food sales over a multiyear period. At some point the Egyptian locals themselves ran out of food and traded their land for indentured servanthood whereby they would work the land (that they no longer owned) and pay Pharaoh 20 percent of the yield.

Once Joseph reunited with his family, Pharaoh invited them to join their brother in Egypt to live. Israel entered Egypt, a wealthy nation. Joseph's father, Jacob, possessed great flocks of cattle and had a large family. Jacob likely inherited a portion of the immense wealth in the form of gold, silver, and cattle passed down from Abraham and Isaac – both wildly successful. Joseph's family would settle in Goshen, raise their cattle, and care for Pharaoh's livestock. Pharaoh considered raising cattle an ignoble task – typically tended to by servants. While the deal for Israel started fine in Egypt (Israel flourished), circumstances began to go downhill as Joseph, Jacob, and the "good Pharaoh" died. Egypt forgot about Joseph and what he did for Egypt and began to fear Israel, forcing them into progressively tougher bondage. Much like today's elite leaders, Pharaoh feared an uprising of the people based on their sheer numbers. At some point, to prevent the tribe of Israel from further expanding, Pharaoh decreed that any boys born into Israel should be killed at birth. Pharaoh invented post birth abortions, eugenics, and population control long before the communists. Pharaoh went after the innocent children.

To Israel, Egypt represented an impenetrable fortress. Israel possessed neither land, rights, nor weapons. Egypt effectively conquered the world using the wisdom given to Joseph and then stole the sweat and labor of the Israelites to build great cities, fortresses, and great pools of assets such as gold and silver. In other words, Egypt used the anointing of God's people to create great wealth for themselves. Subsequently, God raised Moses to deliver Israel, and Moses began to warn Pharaoh of the consequences if he did not let God's people go. Judgment fell on Egypt through ten plagues, including locusts, boils, deadly hail, frogs, and water turning to blood. God's judgment was not for Israel, only Egypt. For instance, one plague killed the livestock of Egypt but did not touch Israel's cattle. God's people were protected from the plagues.

In anger against God's judgment, Egypt persecuted Israel with tougher work conditions, which caused a few complainers to wail against Moses. Today many Christians complain against strong saints exposing the demonic methods of the fourth beast, preferring passivity. In the final plague Israel was directed to cover their doorposts and lintel with lamb's blood so that the death angel would pass over Israel and instead strike the firstborn of the Egyptians, including Pharaoh's son. This blood covering represents a striking example of the ultimate sacrifice of Jesus on the cross.

The events following the final plague were nothing short of miraculous. In Exodus 11:2 (NLT), God commanded Moses, "Tell all the Israelite men and women to ask their Egyptian neighbors for articles of silver and gold." God's divine plan not only included rescuing Israel from slavery but also restoring their wealth. Proverbs 6:31 (AMPC) states, "If [a thief] is found out, he must restore seven times [what he stole]; he must give the whole substance of his house [if necessary – to meet his fine]." Egypt stole Israel's wealth, their ideas, and their labor. They were sick and defeated. As compensation, God gave Israel the gold, silver, and all the cattle of Egypt. God restored their health, wealth, and freedom in divine reparations. This story foreshadows what happens when the fourth beast is defeated – God restores the stolen wealth to His people in divine reparations 2.0 – only this time it will be bigger than in the time of Pharaoh.

After Israel left Egypt, Pharaoh chased Israel into the Red Sea, losing his army when the sea closed in on him, ensuring Israel's enduring freedom. The Bible says, "The Egyptians pursued them, all the horses and chariots of Pharaoh and his horseman and his army" (Ex. 14:9 AMPC). God warned Moses that Pharaoh would come. Pharaoh unwittingly walked into a trap set by God himself. Pharaoh's greed, arrogance, and anger prevailed by God's design. While the buildup to the exodus of Israel took several months, the transfer of wealth and destruction of Egypt occurred in a few days. When the waters covered the Egyptian army, the destruction of Egypt occurred in mere minutes (Ex. 14).

Today we see parallels with the exodus. Humanity serves as slaves to the elite finance system of debt and meager subsistence, despite unlimited world resources. For decades the elites planned the destruction of humanity through a New World Order. As humanity awakes from great slumber, evil plans are evident to all, and mass rejection commences. In war college soldiers learn the concepts of cover and armor. As long as troops retain cover, they don't need armor. However, once a worthy opponent discovers a military position, the cover is lost and it's only a matter of time before armor fails. The evil plans laid for humanity remained largely behind-the-scenes, which gave the enemy cover. Now the cover is blown and humanity knows the players involved. It's only a matter of time before their armor is worn down. Their armor is the finance system that supports and funds evil through bribery and blackmail. Before Pharaoh set out to overtake the Israelites after their exodus, his utter defeat was already determined. The final desperate push to destroy Israel ended up destroying himself and those around him, destroying Egypt.

Bible scholars agree that by taking the shortest path through the desert to the Promise Land of Canaan, a migrant group the size of Israel could conceivably make the journey in only eleven days. Unfortunately, Israel failed to recognize the complete liberation given to them by God and instead resorted to complaining and calling on Moses to return to Egypt. Israel took some of the gold God gave them and crafted a golden calf to worship, openly flaunting God.

God's patience wore thin with Israel, and in Numbers 14:22-23 (Darby), God swore, "all those men who have seen my glory, and my signs, which I did in Egypt and in the wilderness, and have tempted me these ten times, and have not hearkened to my voice, shall in no wise see the land which I did swear unto their fathers: none of them that despised me shall see it." For forty years, Israel marched in circles in the desert, forced to depend on God for daily provision. The heavy gold and silver they carried undoubtedly added to the burden. At the end of the forty years Joshua, Caleb, and a new generation born free proceeded to the promised land.

The first generation of Israel out of slavery possessed great wealth. God supernaturally brought them out of four hundred and thirty years of slavery and offered heavenly reparations, forcing their oppressors to pay dearly. God healed their bodies and showed them open miracles and His glory to win the trust of His people. The slavery Israel came from put them in a mentality that kept them in a state of unbelief – the goodness of God was too much to handle. If the saints are not careful, many of the first generation following the fall of the fourth beast could suffer a similar fate. It's time for the Church to expand its vision and understand the absolute goodness of God. Soldier Saints avoid this error by studying the meaning of poverty mentality and performing a self-assessment on their own lives. Poverty mentality is an attitude often passed between generations. Zig Ziglar noted the focusing on what is missing in one's life rather than focusing on what is there can lead to perpetual poverty. God gave Israel the world wealth and completely set them free from bondage – still they complained. They even expressed a desire to go back to Egypt! Have you ever done something really nice for your child and then he/she complains about a small inconvenience? Soldier Saints are thankful people who get up every day praising God for even the opportunity to live another day. When God performs His mighty work on the fourth beast and you are tempted to complain about an irrelevant detail – remember that God pays attention to our attitude. Speak the Word of God only and adopt a spirit of thankfulness.

Walls of Jericho

After the death of Moses, God gave Joshua orders to cross the Jordan River, and they began to conquer and finally take the land God promised to Abraham, Isaac, and Jacob many years prior. They soon encountered another impenetrable fortress in the city of Jericho. Because of mountainous barriers and an inner and outer protective wall, Jericho, occupied by the Canaanites, withstood many attacks up to the time of Joshua. Joshua sent spies into Jericho to check it out. The spies found refuge in Rahab's home, located in the walls of Jericho. Rahab told the spies why she decided to help them:

> I know that the Lord has given you the land and that your terror is fallen upon us that all the inhabitants of

the land faint because of you. For we have heard how the Lord dried up the water of the Red Sea for you when you came out of Egypt, and what you did to the two kings of the Amorites who were on the [east] side of the Jordan, Sihon and Og, who you utterly destroyed. When we heard it, our hearts melted, neither did spirit or courage remain any more in any man because of you, for the Lord your God, He is God in heaven above and on earth beneath" (Josh. 2:9-11 AMPC).

It's fascinating that Rahab, a harlot (in today's vernacular, a hooker) recognized God's power. She took a risk for Joshua's spies because she recognized God's glory and her own fate if she did not help God's people. God has a sense of humor. I believe He put this story in the Bible to show us that it's the common people, the sinners, that recognize God's glory and take risks for God. When Jesus showed up, the religious order of the day failed to recognize their visitation from God. Jesus chose a bunch of fishermen, tax collectors, and other vagabonds to lead the greatest revolution the planet has seen. Notably absent among Jesus' disciples were members of the Pharisaic order. The only Pharisee that came around later was Paul, who only recognized God after he was knocked off his horse and struck with blindness before he "saw the light"! As a sign that Rahab was protected, the spies asked her to hang a red cord from her window. The red cord represented blood protection from God's judgment, just like the blood on the doors protected the Israelites when the angel of death passed over Egypt. Both are types of the blood of Jesus, which protects saints today from judgment.

Israel did not possess the equipment or military might to topple Jericho, whose walls, combined with the other geographical features, rendered it nearly impregnable. Upon entering the Promised Land after Moses' death, God gave the people a sign that He anointed Joshua to be their leader. When priests began to cross the Jordan River with the Ark of the Covenant, the Jordan dried up supernaturally to let them pass through. On the other side of the river, God directed Joshua again with a simple step of obedience – to circumcise all males yet uncircumcised.

Rather than march right on the city and take heavy casualties, Joshua camped near Jericho and waited for a plan from the Lord. The plan came through an angel who outlined the steps Joshua needed to take to defeat Jericho. The simple plan involved marching around the city once for six days and then marching around the city seven times on the seventh day before giving a great shout unto God. Joshua relayed the plan to the armies and the priests. The people obeyed and Jericho's walls fell on the seventh day, allowing Israel to thoroughly defeat the city. I find it interesting that Joshua then cursed anyone who would seek to rebuild Jericho. Vile practices likely conducted in Jericho meant it should not come back. When the fourth beast is judged, many demonic edifices and structures need to be destroyed forever.

After Jericho's defeat, Israel captured the gold and silver from the city and placed it in the temple treasury. Once again, impenetrable fortresses fell and a wealth transfer occurred. From beginning to end, God fought the battle for Israel. Walls don't normally come down with a shout and horns. No, God used an earthquake or some other miraculous method to bring the walls down. He needed His people to do one thing – obey.

The book of Joshua marked a huge transition point for Israel. Once they crossed the Jordan River, they ate off the land for the first time in forty years. The manna, supernaturally provided daily bread, stopped falling from the sky. God fed Israel manna for forty years in the desert. Now He stopped providing manna, and His people could now enjoy the variety and richness of the fruit of the Promised Land. Most in the camp enjoyed the first outside meal they ever had, having survived on manna for decades. As a sign of meaningful progress on Israel's part, they did not complain about the manna drying up – the poverty mentality broken.

Samarian Seige

In a situation quite opposite of Jericho, Ahab, the king of Israel, now found he and his people trapped in Samaria under a total embargo by King Ben-hadad of Syria. The city and its inhabitants were starving to death. The king in absolute desperation sought to kill Elisha, a mighty prophet of God. We don't have the full account written for us, but perhaps Elisha already informed the king that God would deliver them, and the king began to doubt the prophet because of the delays and the suffering he observed. In 2 Kings 7:1 (AMPC) Elisha replied, "Hear the word of the Lord. Thus says the Lord: Tomorrow about this time a measure of fine flour will sell for a shekel, and two measures of barley for a shekel in the gate of Samaria." Elisha predicted a reversal of fortune, for in the prior chapter, a donkey's head, hardly a delicacy, sold for eighty shekels of silver. The king's captain scoffed at the prophecy, to which Elisha replied, "You will see this but you won't be able to enjoy it" (my paraphrase).

What happened next – a miracle. Four condemned and starving lepers at the gates of Samaria decided they might as well wander into the Syrians' camp because they were destined for death either way. As they approached the Syrian position, God amplified the noise of their footsteps and the Syrian army fled, leaving their silver, gold, and food. Word eventually got back to Ahab, and the city was saved by a glorious miracle. The king's captain died after being trampled underfoot by the stampede, leaving the city to find food and water.

The Samarian siege once again proves even when circumstances are dire and the enemy seems insurmountable, God easily turns things around. In this case, God worked with a few desperate lepers who possessed the courage to march toward the Syrians. God amplified their footsteps mightily, such that the enemies fled in horror.

Babylon, The Great Fortress

After Israel cycled through times of both obedience and betrayal many times, they finally stooped to complete idolatry and fell to Babylon under King Nebuchadnezzar, who destroyed Jerusalem and its temple and openly mocked the Jewish faith and instruments of worship. Historians believe the Babylonians destroyed the temple around 586 BC. Israel's leaders were instructed by the prophets not to resist and to submit to Babylon. The Babylonians exiled most of the remaining Jews to Babylon as slaves. Daniel, among the children carried off by the Babylonians, served in the king's court. He ended up writing much on the End Times and was the first prophet to reveal how history would unfold for several thousand years in the future. Ironically, we still live under one of the four beast systems Daniel described when he accurately divined a king's dream thousands of years ago.

Again the Israelites found themselves slaves to an ungodly and satanic empire that built a mighty fortress to defend itself. The

Babylonians built an impenetrable fortress city as its capital. Great walls surrounded the Babylonian capital, built higher and thicker than any prevailing military technologies could penetrate. Always several steps ahead, God devised a plan to topple Babylon before its formation. His prophets spoke of a leader named Cyrus (also known by other names) some two hundred years before Cyrus's birth. Isaiah and others spoke of Cyrus as a coming king who would not expressly know God but would be good to Israel. Some scholars believe that Cyrus found inspiration in the writings about himself in Isaiah and found the courage to move against the Babylonians as a result. Cyrus first defeated the Babylonians on the open battlefield. Following their loss, the Babylonians retreated into the safety of their walled city. Believing their impenetrable city protected them, the Babylonians mocked God by drinking from stolen golden chalices once used in the Hebrew temple worship. Unbeknownst to the Babylonians, Cyrus, with the assistance of four other national armies, launched a Biblical special-forces operation. In a second battle, Cyrus's forces entered the impenetrable Babylonian city through the drainage system and defeated Babylon from the inside of the city. Once again, God thwarted Satan's plan. Israel eventually rebuilt the temple but never again achieved the dominant world status they carried after the time of Egypt and during the reigns of kings David and Solomon.

While no specific wealth was transferred to the Jews after Cyrus defeated Babylon, it's worth noting certain aspects of the story. First, God once again dealt with an impenetrable fortress in a supernatural way, delivering victory in a single day event. Second, God employed a non-believer liberator to achieve victory for Israel. Cyrus, a fierce warrior who fought and won many vicious battles, would not be welcome in a lot of church circles today. Second only to Abraham or Moses, Cyrus fulfilled a critical role for the Israelites. Isaiah prophesied this about Cyrus:

> God's Message to his anointed,
> > to Cyrus, whom he took by the hand
> To give the task of taming the nations,
> > of terrifying their kings –
> He gave him free rein,
> > no restrictions:
> "I'll go ahead of you,
> > clearing and paving the road.
> I'll break down bronze city gates,
> > smash padlocks, kick down barred entrances.
> I'll lead you to buried treasures,
> > secret caches of valuables –
> Confirmations that it is, in fact, I, God,
> > the God of Israel, who calls you by your name.
> It's because of my dear servant Jacob,
> > Israel my chosen,
> That I've singled you out, called you by name,
> > and given you this privileged work.
> > And you don't even know me! (Isa. 45:1-5 MSG)

The Israelites did not pick Cyrus as the vessel to liberate them from Babylon – God picked Cyrus! Cyrus likely possessed crazy character flaws and other issues. However, something about the evil of Babylon did not sit right with Cyrus, and he fought Babylon relentlessly. As the fourth beast is taken down, there will be many saints directly involved. However, there will likely be Cyrus-like people, who may not know God but are as horrified as the saints by the evil the fourth beast represents and will fight to the death for freedom. As saints, we must recognize a righteous anointing on modern-day Cyrus's and embrace them.

Modern-Day Cyrus

When Donald Trump became president in 2016, some modern-day prophets boldly proclaimed President Trump the modern-day King Cyrus. Many of these prophecies went public two-plus years before Trump came to office. I don't believe it's coincidental that Trump became our forty-fifth president! Intrigued by the comparison of President Trump with King Cyrus, I studied Isaiah 45 many times, as well as other passages in the Bible describing King Cyrus. I finally asked the Lord why it appeared that President Trump's work got cut short if he represented the modern-day version of Cyrus. In Isaiah 45, Cyrus possesses incredible power to break through forces, discover hidden treasures, and humiliate kings. The ancient Cyrus completed his work, but Trump did not. The Lord showed me that Cyrus neither defeated Babylon in a single battle nor alone. The decisive victory over Babylon came later as several other nations joined Cyrus to defeat the Babylonian capital in a special-forces, underground operation. At least three other nations joined Cyrus in the effort for the final battle with Babylon. I believe when the fourth beast is defeated and we are afforded insight into the details, we will see that Trump played an extremely valuable part in recruiting other world leaders in bringing down the fourth beast system. We will likely see more of Donald Trump in the future.

God never changes. He took down pagan rulers in the time of old and He possesses the power to do it again. The reparations of wealth to Israel after their miraculous deliverance from bondage and slavery under Egypt is a small taste of what God plans to do with the fourth beast on behalf of His Church. If God did it for Israel, He will do it for us. Begin to speak to your school, city, state or nation and command the walls of bondage to come down. Begin to declare boldly that all things done in darkness will come to light. Command Satan to get his hands off your family and finances. Begin to thank God in advance for the work He is doing to tear down the fourth beast strongholds. Pray for God to reveal His destiny for you as a Soldier Saint in the Kingdom Age of the Saints. Only be strong as you wait for God's answer.

"I believe Soldier Saints that boldly believe God and demonstrate courage to stand up to fourth beast tyranny will be given the most responsibility in the Kingdom Age of the Saints."

– Benjamin Thomas

9. The Revelation Riddle

Blessed is the one who reads the words of God's message, and blessed are the people who hear this message and do what is written in it. The time is near when all of this will happen.
– *Rev 1:3 NCV*

Did you know the Bible mentions that those who read the book of Revelation get a special blessing? When I was growing up, reading the book of Revelation compared to stepping in an anthill. It caused a lot of discomfort and panic, but eventually, I got through it. In the first few chapters, Jesus addresses seven churches and discusses both victories and flaws, with specific exhortation and correction given to each church. Revelation 3 reminds us that Jesus would rather we be cold or hot because He rejects lukewarm Christians.

The Revelation Riddle serves as a guide for Soldier Saints – a picture of the future. We are to believe, expect, and claim our rightful place during this special age. Many won't understand the Revelation Riddle until after the leadership positions are filled in the Kingdom Age of the Saints – so many are tied to their rescue rapture theology and slavery mentality. Under the fourth beast, we experienced slavery for so long many are unable to absorb the goodness of God due to poverty mentality. I recently attempted to convince a man mightily used of God in revival that God's plan for us in the End Times was better than we thought. He could not see it. In fact he angrily challenged me. The fact is only two of twelve of the Israelite spies possessed the promised land – 17 percent mathematically. I hope that more than 17 percent of the body of Christ possess the modern-day promised land, but I am not sure it will happen. Will you be among the 17 percent of believers who possess the promised land? My hearts' desire is everyone that reads this book grab onto the promises and help lead in the Kingdom Age of the Saints. I want every saint to participate – God's goodness amazes me. He's better and more generous than we even knew. My heart yearns for God's people to recognize His goodness, His kindness, and His generosity. He is the Good Father.

The Kingdom Age in the Book of Revelation

In studying the book of Revelation for clues about the Kingdom Age of the Saints, it initially seemed to me that Daniel provided more background on this special age. Daniel 7 mentions the kingdom (reign) being given to the saints in multiple instances. But the book of Revelation provides insight into the Kingdom Age of the Saints, hidden in riddle form. According to *The Century Dictionary and Cyclopedia*, a riddle is a proposition framed to exercise one's ingenuity in discovering its meaning; an ambiguous, complex, or puzzling question offered for a solution; an enigma; a dark saying. In addition to speaking to His people in parables, Jesus also provides riddles in His Word that must be unlocked.

Every time Jesus addresses a church in the book of Revelation, He ends with a seemingly out-of-place promise. For instance, in Revelation 2 Jesus exhorts the Church of Ephesus. He points out that the Ephesian church loves truth but abandoned its first love. Then He ends speaking to Ephesus in verse 7 (CEV) with "I will let everyone who wins the victory eat from the life-giving tree in God's wonderful garden." This Scripture seems wildly out of place, moving from speaking to Ephesus to speaking more broadly to the Church about overcoming and eating once again from the tree of life mentioned in the Garden of Eden.

In the passages that follow, Jesus provides additional provocative and seemingly out-of-place promises, constituting fragments of a powerful message. By placing the promises together in a single paragraph, the text emerges:

- "I will let everyone who wins the victory eat from the life-giving tree in God's wonderful garden." (v. 7)

- "Whoever wins the victory will not be hurt by the second death." (v. 11)

- "To everyone who wins the victory, I will give some of the hidden food [manna]. I will also give each one a white stone with a new name written on it. No one will know that name except the one who is given the stone." (v. 17)

- "I will give power over the nations to everyone who wins the victory and keeps on obeying me until the end. I will give each of them the same power my Father has given me. They will rule the nations with an iron rod and smash those nations to pieces like clay pots. I will also give them the morning star." (vv. 26-28)

- "Everyone who wins the victory will wear white clothes. Their names will not be erased from the book of life, and I will tell my Father and his angels that they are my followers." (Rev 3:5)

- "Everyone who wins the victory will be made into a pillar in the temple of my God, and they will stay there forever. I will write on each of them the name of my God and the name of his city. It is the new Jerusalem my God will send down from heaven. I will also write on them my own new name." (v. 12)

- "Everyone who wins the victory will sit with me on my throne, just as I won the victory and sat with my Father on his throne." (v. 21)

I believe the remarkable riddle uncovered in Revelation speaks to the Kingdom Age of the Saints. For one thing, each promise starts with a condition of winning the victory. Other translations speak to "overcoming" or "conquering." The saints won't need to overcome when we arrive in heaven – there is no devil in heaven to overcome. When the Bible speaks of overcoming, it's tied to overcoming in the world. First John 5:4-5 (NCV) states, "Everyone who is a child of God conquers the world. And this is the victory that conquers the world – our faith. So the one who conquers the world is the person who believes that Jesus is the Son of God." We won't need to overcome or conquer during the millennial reign of Christ when Satan is locked up and Jesus rules the world in the flesh. The riddle speaks to a special age when saints overcome the world and rule the nations. The Revelation riddle describes certain facets of the kingdom age that provide more color and detail than the book of Daniel.

Understanding the Revelation Riddle

Longevity

The Revelation riddle starts with the first promise related to the tree of life. The tree of life is mentioned as a specific tree in the Garden of Eden. Eating of the tree of life grants longevity. After Adam and Eve both ate of the fruit of the knowledge, the Lord said in Genesis 3:22 (CEV), "They now know the difference between right and wrong, just as we do. But they must not be allowed to eat fruit from the tree that lets them live forever." Remember, the death of the fourth beast will purge our food supply and environment of carcinogenic toxins. We will rediscover ancient medicine related to herbs, spices, weeds, roots, and other healthy pharmaceutical alternatives. Healthy living and a clean environment certainly should extend the life span of humanity by a few years. However, the Revelation riddle describes longevity during the kingdom age that can only be explained by walking in divine health or perhaps new technology enabling humans to live longer. In early Biblical days, men and women lived hundreds of years. Methuselah, the longest living person recorded in Biblical history, lived nearly one thousand years (Gen. 5:27).

The second part of the Revelation riddle mentions that "Whoever wins the victory will not be hurt by the second death." Because the kingdom age precedes the Rapture and the marriage supper of the Lamb, many saints living in the kingdom age will not experience bodily death. The term *second death* refers to bodily death; the first death relates to spiritual death when men and women reach the age of accountability when they lose their initial innocence and make a decision to follow Jesus or not. Paul discusses this concept in Romans 7:9 (ESV), "I was once alive apart from the law, but when the commandment came, sin came alive and I died." The Bible also describes the second death as the lake of fire, which is the final destination for unbelievers and Satan himself after a great and final day of judgment.

Wealth

The third promise in the Revelation riddle refers to a new form of hidden manna given to the overcomers. Jesus promises, "I will give some of the hidden manna to everyone who wins the victory. I will also give to each one who wins the victory a white stone with a new name written on it. No one knows this new name except the one who receives it" (Rev 2:17 NCV). Manna, a miraculous flaky honey bread that fell from the sky, provided nourishment to Israel during their time in the desert after they were liberated from Egypt. After the morning dew, manna lay on the ground, and Israel was commanded to store only enough for a single day because anything extra would spoil. Israel never once worried about food and provision – God provided them daily bread supernaturally.

I believe the hidden manna spoken of in the Revelation riddle includes technology greatly beneficial to humanity but purposely hidden to maximize profits for fourth beast merchants. The Revelation riddle goes on to say that overcomers will be given a stone with a new name that only the recipient knows. This stone, related to the concept of manna, is something that contains monetary value but is durable. Blockchain technology, which represents a decentralized, permanent record of transactions, may explain the white stone in the Revelation riddle. When a person sets up a self-custody digital wallet on the blockchain, each user is given a new twelve to twenty-four word passphrase unique to the user's wallet. Only the owner of the wallet knows the passphrase. Many digital assets, such as the Ripple XRP utility token, can be stored in a cold wallet that the user can take with them anywhere and exchange their digital assets for fiat currency and otherwise trade at very low rates. Other digital assets like equities and bonds are tokenized on networks like the Stellar Exchange. If a digital wallet is lost, users may restore their holdings simply by utilizing their secret passcode. As fourth beast assets are seized, I believe these assets are tokenized on the blockchain for transfer to saints' digital wallets.

New digital currencies are expected to be backed by commodities, such as gold and silver, yielding stable value with little inflation risk. In the future, all assets such as homes, cars, land, equities, and bonds will be given an immutable serial number on the blockchain, providing people to trade with each other without intermediaries in a decentralized manner. For many years, large companies such as IBM, Deloitte, and others built critical technology to ensure scalability and ubiquitous access to the various digital exchanges. In a recent discussion on distributed ledger technology, Richard Walker, a partner at Bain & Company, predicted trillions of dollars of value would flow into blockchain-based digital assets over the next decade.[95] When current, illiquid assets become tokenized on the blockchain, immense opportunities for wealth creation are created that bypass entrenched intermediaries tied to current banking systems, who scrape enormous fees from transactions. Perhaps these are mechanisms we will use during the Kingdom Age of the Saints, related to the hidden manna Jesus discusses in the Revelation riddle.

When God blesses His people, He adds no sorrow to the blessing. This truth provides clues for saints to discern between digital control by a satanic system versus the freedom of self-custody wallets by a pure system designed to benefit humanity. Any digital currency that requires indelible chips under the skin represents a satanic system. Many saints are now drawn to the digital asset world at the same time globalist banking leaders are also talking about digital IDs and Central Bank Digital Currencies. Saints can distinguish the difference by the level of privacy invasion and control any new system renders.

Geopolitical Control

The fourth promise in the Revelation riddle speaks directly to ruling and reigning on earth. Revelation 2:26-28 (CEV) states, "I will give power over the nations to everyone who wins the victory and keeps on obeying me until the end. I will give each of them the same power my Father has given me. They will rule the nations with an

---

95   Richard Walker and Patrick O'Meara, "Delivering Enterprise-Grade Digital Solutions to Global Markets and Investors," *YouTube*, June 1, 2023, https://www.youtube.com/watch?v=9PCsRy1l8LI.

iron rod and smash those nations to pieces like clay pots. I will also give them the morning star."

These two verses are packed with important promises. Saints in the kingdom age are given power over the nations to rule with an iron rod and to smash nations (or governments) to pieces. The fourth beast system represents the longest reigning satanic empire in history. The fourth beast maintains the rule of the nations today through the banking and governance system. In the Kingdom Age of the Saints the rule and reign of the nations is given to the saints. The saints smash these godless institutions.

In the Revelation riddle we learn which saints are eligible to rule the nations. Jesus specifically states it's the saints who win the victory (over Satan) and *continue* to be obedient to Jesus until the end. Enduring and unflappable saints who refuse to compromise and are not changed by wealth will possess lasting positions of influence and rule over the nations. Flaky saints, who digress and backslide when wealth is placed into their hands, are not eligible to rule. Note that saints rule the nations with an iron rod. God raises saints intolerant of evil and dedicated to righteous rule. Jesus refers to the power to rule as a power He received from His Father, which He then gives to the saints during the kingdom age. When Jesus says, "I give him the morning star," a term used in the Bible to describe Jesus Himself, He is saying, "I give you my authority." To remove doubt that He possessed this authority, Jesus said to His disciples, "Do you suppose that I cannot appeal to My Father, and He will immediately provide Me with more than twelve legions of angels?" (Matt. 26:53 AMPC). Jesus possesses authority over the angels with the power to destroy demonic strongholds on earth. However, Jesus chose to forgo geopolitical reign, recognizing the fourth beast's lease on earth remained for another couple of thousand years. Now, however, we see Jesus giving the saints the ability to rule and judge during the Kingdom Age of the Saints, perhaps with angelic assistance.

Soldier Saints

In the fifth section of the Revelation riddle, Jesus promises, "Everyone who wins the victory will wear white clothes. Their names will not be erased from the book of life, and I will tell my Father and his angels that they are my followers" (Rev 3:5 CEV). Here Jesus discusses the righteous aspect of the ruling saints in the kingdom age. Dressed in white, the saints know who they are, their names are recorded in the book of life, and Jesus is proud of them, declaring their names before the Father and the angels. Soldier Saints are very special in the sight of God. Soldier Saints are intercessory prayer warriors, moms showing up at school board meetings, and entrepreneurs providing awesome, healthy alternatives to big agriculture and big pharma. Soldier Saints are soldiers who recite Psalm 91 before entering into a dark hole, ready to root out child traffickers by force.

Victory Trophies in Heaven

In the sixth section, we read, "Everyone who wins the victory will be made into a pillar in the temple of my God, and they will stay there forever. I will write on each of them the name of my God and the name of his city. It is the new Jerusalem my God will send down from heaven. I will also write on them my own new name" (Rev 3:12 CEV). The Soldier Saints who take down the fourth beast and rule the world during the Kingdom Age of the Saints possess a legacy going forward in the annals of heaven. We know that the twelve leaders of the twelve tribes of Israel and the twelve disciples are sitting on thrones around God's throne. But now we learn there are victory pillars in the temple of God, presumably named after Soldier Saints. The names of the saints contributing to the takedown of the fourth beast are added to great patrons of war already on victory pillars, including King David, Moses, Samson, and others. Jesus writes on the Soldier Saints the name of God, the name of the city of God. This speaks to either a special crown in heaven awarded to the individuals or some other marking designating victorious warriors involved in special operations for the kingdom of God. In Hebrews 11, we are given a documentary of the faith hall of fame. According to Scripture, God prepares a Kingdom Age of the Saints hall of fame in heaven and also in the new Jerusalem.

Time of Rest and Joy

The seventh section of the Revelation riddle reads, "Everyone who wins the victory will sit with me on my throne, just as I won the victory and sat with my Father on his throne" (Rev 3:21 CEV). Even God Himself enjoyed a day of rest on the seventh day of creation. A time of rest is promised to the Soldier Saints when they earn the honor of sitting with Jesus on His throne and resting from the work of overcoming. Often misinterpreted, Biblical suffering is the exhausting labor, along with the resulting persecution, required to resist the devil as long as he roams earth.

First Peter 5:9 (NLT) states, "Stand firm against him [Satan], and be strong in your faith. Remember that your family of believers all over the world is going through the same kind of suffering you are". Jesus spent time during His ministry warding off continuous attacks from religious leaders and other demonically oppressed people. Jesus walked in victory, but the fact that He fought battles along the way, including persecution, is the type of suffering that bold Soldier Saints must endure.

Paul suffered intense persecution, and soothsayers and demon-possessed people continuously disrupted his meetings. Right now the Church is weary of fighting. We are attacked on every front and are expected to hold the line. It's not easy, and our Father understands. In the Revelation riddle, He promises a time of rest for the overcomer. It paints a picture of Jesus sitting down and resting on His Father's throne when death, hell, and the grave were defeated after the cross, when Jesus' assignment to save humanity was completed and the temple's curtain ripped from top to bottom. A moment is coming when the geopolitical forces ruling our planet are finished and the work of restoring order on our planet is complete. Then peace and rest come for the Soldier Saints along with recognition in heaven.

Soldier Saints internalize the Revelation riddle and ask God how they can experience God's best in their own lives. Soldier Saints desire to experience all of what God offers and stay in their prayer room until they walk out with God's gifts. Look to your children for an example. Parents stock the house with food and supplies. Children then access these blessings when hungry. Few parents put a padlock on the refrigerator. We love our children and don't take offense to their boldness (unless they eat a whole gallon of ice cream). God exudes the perfect father – He wants His children to be excited about His plans and actively participate. Stir up a childlike hunger for all God offers to you. Develop an innocent curiosity for God's gifts. He loves it when His children ask questions and "become childlike". Become like "curious George" when it comes to God's ways, anointing and gifts – only be courageous.

10. The World Under the Saints

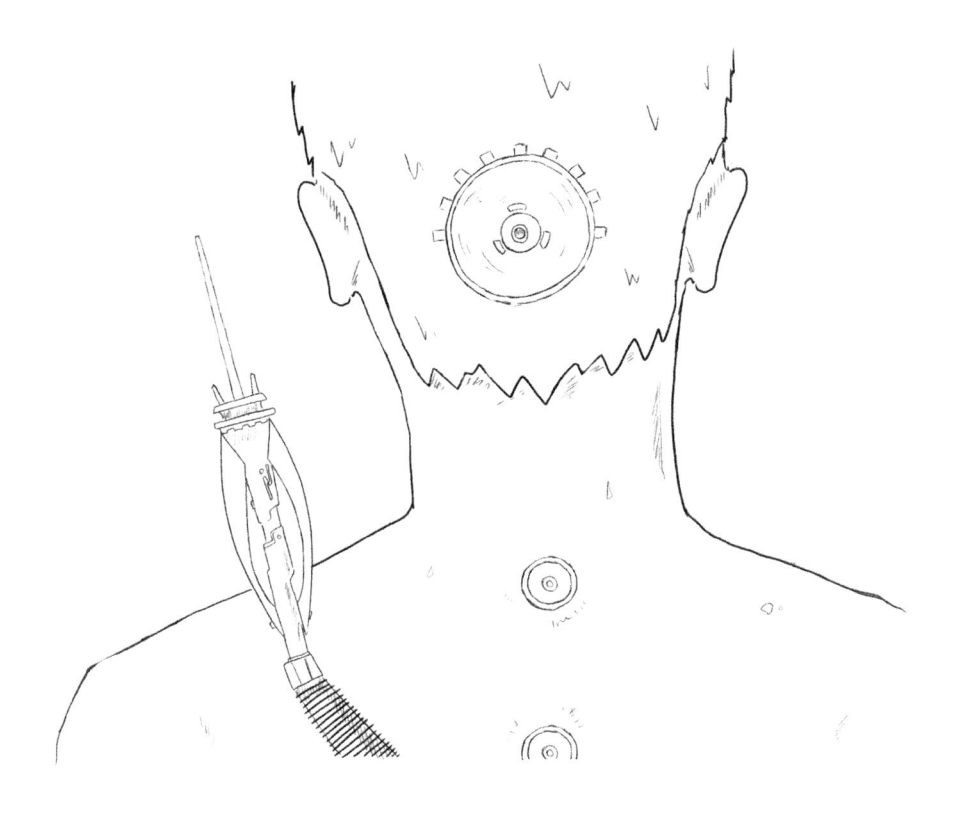

When the godly are in authority, the people rejoice. But when the wicked are in power, they groan.
— *Prov 29:2 NLT*

How do we prepare to reign and rule in this special age? Start by putting away the rescue rapture mat – you won't need it. The Rapture comes before the dragon appears on the scene, likely hundreds of years in the future. The Rapture occurs to reunite the victorious Church with Jesus for a time of celebration. Remember Enoch in the Old Testament? God took Enoch to heaven without physical death because He enjoyed his fellowship – Enoch pleased

God (Heb. 11:5). Stop looking for places to hide and instead look for places to lead. If you don't fear the fourth beast, he possesses no power over you. The fourth beast controlled Christians for hundreds of years through fear. Jesus did not walk in fear during His earthly ministry, despite living under the same fourth beast rule. He got His orders from the Holy Spirit in prayer and moved forward in obedience and absolute authority over Satan.

Close your eyes and start to imagine a world no longer under the dominion of the fourth beast. Fourth beast control over the seven pillars of society soon comes to an end. When the fourth beast is slain, the seven pillars radically change under the leadership of the saints. Let the Lord show you how you participate in rebuilding our society, under the guidance of the Holy Spirit. You made it to chapter ten – God calls you to be an active participant in the Kingdom Age of the Saints.

Hopefully, God already began to speak to you. You see, God needs the hands and feet of the body of Christ to accomplish His mission in the earth. The degree to which He can use us corresponds to our obedience. God does not need intellect, although if accompanied by childlike faith and humility, intellect helps. God can give His children wisdom, as He endowed Solomon. Your number one asset is obedience. You see, God used donkeys to prophecy in the Bible. He desires servants which follow Him precisely to accomplish great things in the earth. In the study guide that accompanies this book, I show how God used many unsuspecting individuals in the Bible to accomplish supernatural objectives. All saw themselves as quite ordinary. I also provide tools and frameworks to prepare Soldier Saints for what's coming. I encourage you to dig into the material to help you prepare for the Kingdom Age of the Saints.

Government

Government became a massive tool of the fourth beast, swelling to ten times the size needed to function. As private central banks rolled out worldwide, governments came under the control of the fourth beast system. To control government leaders, private central banks wielded a powerful weapon: by decreasing the money supply, preplanned recessions occurred. By increasing the money supply, the private central banks caused inflation and bubbles leading to market crashes. Government leaders who fought private central banks were removed and replaced by well-funded, compliant officials. The bankers forced large loans on governments, who spent money on behemoth agencies controlling the masses through regulation and perverse incentives.

Governments became corporations motivated by profit rather than public service. Major corporations, through partnerships with government, figured out how to transfer business risks to the taxpayers, allowing the corporations to maximize profit. For example, in 2008 the U.S. banking industry transferred billions of dollars of worthless mortgage-backed securities to taxpayers while retaining productive assets for themselves, increasing the national debt. In addition, the cycle of federalizing whole industries at the taxpayers' expense and then subsequently privatizing the same industries at a discount for the benefit of elite cronies is a further example of fleecing the taxpayer. The debts of governments continue to explode, despite the adverse effects on citizens, their children, and grandchildren.

When the fourth beast is slain, everything changes. The size of governments drastically reduces and government merely plays the role of shared public service, providing a fair and equitable justice system and a limited military. The people enjoy more discretionary income following deep tax cuts. The people empower governments to serve, focused on maintaining roads, bridges, and public parks. A restoration of equal justice occurs as institutions revert to their original charters. Local laws are enforced by officers with integrity who serve justice to corrupt judges and attorneys. Free and fair elections are restored, according to the people's will. The original American republic is restored, based on the Constitution and Bill of Rights. Citizens once again understand the American Constitution and Bill of Rights are modeled on the Bible. While the American republic is copied around the world, some countries instead choose to be ruled by benevolent kings who love their people. National sovereignty and a love and respect for one's own rich cultural roots are restored. Orchestrated immigration and the removal of national borders ceases – recognized as a plan hatched by the fourth beast to demoralize nations. The nation of Israel will be freed from the grips of the Khazarians.

Worldwide, most people desire to live in peace and raise their families with purpose. When the saints are in charge, we experience incredible peace on earth. Gone are the days of government-sponsored false-flag operations leading to unnecessary wars and bloodshed. The fourth beast historically thrived and prospered through conflict – fomenting wars and keeping people in fear. The fourth beast system won't survive and therefore cannot plan and initiate wars. The true saints, led by the Spirit of God, are not motivated by an insatiable lust for power, requiring conflict and misery to achieve a redistribution of assets to their balance sheets. The true saints of God want peace, using their resources to help others.

Family

The nuclear family endured unrelenting attacks by the fourth beast for decades. Beginning in the 1970s and 1980s, television shows emerged depicting fathers as bumbling idiots failing to garner respect from their children. More recently television shows normalize gay parents and blended families. Strong men in particular are noticeably absent in today's television and cinema programming. Organizations espousing a nuclear family are demonized and attacked by the media. The American Black community, which in the 1930s and 1940s had the lowest divorce rates in the United States, was decimated by government-sponsored welfare programs that reduced incentives for young Blacks to prosper. The media vilifies true role models for young people, such as Dr. Ben Carson, who grew up in a single-mother home to become a famous surgeon. The media celebrates gangster rappers who abuse drugs while rapping about killing cops. As a result of the welfare system and lack of true role models, crime rates rose in Black communities, and now most Black children are raised by single mothers.

The fourth beast handlers introduced the concept of women's liberation to cause women to feel inferior as homemakers and mothers. Now both adult members of the family work to support the home. As inflation and prices increased, two incomes became a necessity for most families in the United States. To make it work, parents put children in daycare for most of the day, often leading to behavior problems. New pediatric diagnoses, such as attention deficit syndrome, are routinely treated with pharmaceuticals. Divorce rates skyrocketed in America even among Christians, leading to broken and mixed families. This new normal is not God's design. Children raised in a loving home, mentored by both parents with a Biblical worldview, will be productive members of society and are far less likely to fall victim to crime. Programming and imagery in today's media and entertainment show an opposite picture of God's plan for the family.

Business

Under the fourth beast a handful of major corporations and elite families own most of the earth's natural resources, manufacturing, and service businesses. Resource-rich nations in Africa and Latin America are regularly pillaged by mining and production companies who bribe local leaders and leave local citizens penniless and hungry. Many giant corporations access government subsidies, giving them an unfair advantage and making it difficult for small businesses to compete. Despite the existence of government agencies supposedly formed to protect local environments, major corporations poison entire communities and pay only small fines while small businesses are regulated out of existence. Government officials enter office with limited net worth but leave with millions of dollars of net worth. The unholy alliance between government and big business is part of the fourth beast system.

Many leaders of major corporations belong to secret societies and pledge allegiance to the fourth beast system. With Satan as the spiritual leader, the system focuses on destroying humanity, the prize creation of God. Cancer-causing poisons such as glyphosate, the world's most popular chemical, lace our food – 93 percent of Americans were found to have glyphosate residues in their urine.[96] Major beverage manufacturers soak up the available water supplies

---

96 Max Goldberg, "Our Food Is Being Poisoned by Toxic Chemicals – Here's What You Can Do to Protect Yourself," *Detox Project,* August 28, 2017, https://detoxproject.org/food-poisoned-toxic-chemicals-heres-can-protect.

in Africa and other poor continents and serve it back to citizens in the form of diabetes and sickness-causing corn syrup drinks.[97] Processed foods, served by fast-food joints but also available at grocery stores, are laced with metallic toxins and harmful artificial flavoring.[98] Harmful radiation saturates our environments through 5G radio towers installed without the permission of local citizens.[99] Geo-engineering poisons our skies with aluminum and other toxins in the name of protecting the environment.[100] Industrial toxins and fluoride, now proven to be carcinogenic, are added to our water, attack brain function, and damage fertility.[101] With the help of the government, the world healthcare system substituted toxic hydrocarbon-based drugs for natural remedies available in nature.[102] True cures for cancer and other ailments are suppressed and regulated out of existence, while damaging pharmaceuticals with marginal success rates and harmful side effects are promoted nonstop. It seems like every other commercial on TV promotes drugs directly to consumers.

Upon the death of the fourth beast, businesses will change radically. The wealth stolen by the fourth beast elite will return to the people. The private central bank system will be replaced with a transparent, decentralized system. The spending power of money

---

[97] Leslie Ridgeway, "High Fructose Corn Syrup Linked to Diabetes," *USC News*, November 28, 2012, https://news.usc.edu/44415/high-fructose-corn-syrup-linked-to-diabetes
[98] "Are You Eating Foods High in Heavy Metals?" *Outside*, March 1, 2020, https://www.betternutrition.com/diet-and-nutrition/foods-high-in-heavy-metals.
[99] Miroslava Karaboytcheva, "European Parliament Briefing: Effects of 5G Wireless Communication on Human Health," (EMF)SA, February 2020, https://www.emfsa.co.za/news/european-parliament-briefing-effects-of-5g-wireless-communication-on-human-health/
[100] Dane Wigington, "Geoengineering Watch: Our First Ever High Altitude Atmospheric Testing," *GeoEngineering Watch*, November 19, 2020, https://www.geoengineeringwatch.org/geoengineering-watch-our-first-ever-high-altitude-atmospheric-testing/
[101] Jack Kall and Griffin Cole, "Fluoride Toxicity: Exposure, Effects, and Examples," *IAOMT*, accessed June 21, 2023, https://iaomt.org/resources/fluoride-facts/fluoride-toxicity-exposure-effects.
[102] Rodney Howard-Browne and Paul L. Williams, *The Phantom Virus: How an Unseen Enemy Shut Down the Planet!* (Tampa, FL, River Publishing, 2020), 21-22.

based on hard assets will go further without degrading in value week by week due to inflation. Household savings will endure, and a single household income will remain sufficient for most homes. Tax-funded incentives for major corporations will cease. National resources will enrich the local citizens and not the balance sheets of mining and resource giants controlled by the fourth beast. Citizens will no longer need to study every food label for hidden poison. Fast-food chains will change their practices to serve nutritious food or go out of business. Technologies will be released to clean up our environment, soil, and water, allowing the production of healthy food once again. Small businesses will thrive worldwide, boosted by a reduction of government regulation. Entrepreneurs will improve their communities without the risk of getting shut down by governments or big business. Most government-sponsored business will cease as governments are relegated to the lowest form of shared public service, by and for the people.

Technologies hidden from the public that would otherwise benefit humanity at the expense of big business will be released. Our standard of living will increase as new energy production technologies not reliant on burning hydrocarbons are released. The release of new healthcare technologies not reliant on dirty hydrocarbon-based drugs will render most Western-style medicine obsolete. Humanity will rediscover the healing power of herbs, plants, and wholesome foods.

Media

The fourth beast control of the media and entertainment business is critical to maintaining credibility among the public. Stories exposing the corruption of government are regularly buried. Villains and liars are celebrated, and true heroes are ignored. False-flag events are carefully broadcast to instill maximum fear. We are told what and who to believe. Recent massive protests against government overreach in France, Germany, Brazil, and China received limited mainstream media coverage. The media remains virtually silent on takedowns of pedophile and child-trafficking rings. The news cycle, designed to keep citizens in fear, rarely exposes government and corporate corruption. The talking heads at many mainstream media outlets have lied about so many things, I adopt the opposite position by default.

The fourth beast also controls the entertainment industry. Movies and television shows void of morality continue to degrade in quality. To distract able-bodied people, the fourth beast created an elaborate professional sports industry. While many spent their free time on sports, the fourth beast quietly plotted to dominate the pillars of society, virtually unopposed. We exchange meaningless sports scores, outcomes, and championship winners. Captivated by sports, millions of Christians fail to use this time to get involved on school boards or in politics, spend time with their children, or learn new skills. Mocking fans, the professional sports teams embraced the recent kneeling of players during the U.S. national anthem and also embraced the Black Lives Matter organization, a known Marxist group.[103] Riddled with satanic imagery, the Super Bowl half-time shows and Olympic games ridicule Christian ideals. The fourth beast taunts Christians spending hours tuned into the games. Early Roman leaders learned to pacify the people by sponsoring games in large

---

[103] James Simpson, "The roots of Black Lives Matter unveiled", *AIM Center for Investigative Journalism*, January 16, 2016, https://www.influencewatch.org/app/uploads/2017/08/WND-The-roots-of-Black-Lives-Matter-unveiled.pdf

amphitheaters. Emperor Nero stepped it up a notch by torturing Christians in the arenas. Not much has changed in modern times.

Following the death of the fourth beast, humanity will rekindle an insatiable appetite for truth. Slowly, the scales of decades of brainwashing and falsehoods will lift from the people who no longer believe lies. Independent news sources, led by lovers of truth, will skyrocket in popularity. Independent filmmakers will retell the wonderful stories of the Bible. The true history of civilization, expressed in new movies and elaborated in vivid detail, will cause massive box-office success. Defunct Hollywood studios will be acquired for very little capital as the saints transform the industry.

Education

The fourth beast infiltrated the education system to create workers to serve major corporations. At a young age, children are taught not to question authority. As children progress through the system and reach college age, they are taught to get a good job. The top business schools teach students that companies cannot be efficient if they don't borrow money, a worldly principle of debt slavery. Relatively few business schools encourage students to start a business. At Harvard Business School, less than 10 percent of MBA graduates found new companies.[104] Our finest minds are encouraged to lend their talents to major corporations.

History taught from a fourth beast perspective carefully glosses over key events that shaped humanity. Fatalistic philosophies from godless thinkers are taught as truth, while Biblical teachings are ignored or ridiculed. The challenges and victories of the founding

---

104 John Byrne, "Why Harvard Business School Didn't Make the Top Ten of This New Entrepreneurship Ranking," *Forbes*, November 1, 2019, https://www.forbes.com/sites/poetsandquants/2019/11/01/why-harvard-business-school-didnt-make-the-top-ten-of-this-new-entrepreneurship-ranking/?sh=33a144db24eb

fathers of America are no longer taught in U.S. public schools. The dangers of communism and socialism are no longer on the syllabus. Children are taught that the world is running out of resources, a satanic lie. Toddlers start out color blind, playing innocently with children of various skin colors but are soon divided into racial groups. Critical race theory, racial propaganda that seeks to divide us, is now taught in public schools. In the last decade children are taught to question their gender. With few exceptions children graduate public school brainwashed, confused, and unable to win in life.

When the saints take over the education system, we will restore classical education and teach our children to explore, create, and live victoriously in life. We will eliminate confusing and ineffective Common Core Curriculum and other propaganda. The history books will be rewritten to explain the fourth beast's rise to power. We will teach our children how to recognize satanic ideas and prevent the infiltration and overthrow of the seven pillars of society. The true history of humanity along with other amazing scientific proofs of God's Word will be taught once again. The Bible, a book that impacted western civilization like no other book ever published, comes back into our schools.

Government grant-based funding for sinister and godless university research will dry up. Our elite U.S. universities founded to teach students about God's Word and His creation either return to their roots or will cease to exist, replaced by new universities. "Safe spaces" will disappear as exposure of the corrupt system and events leading to its downfall are discussed and debated for generations to come. True heroes of our society will be celebrated and discussed, including evangelists who introduced the gospel to the unchurched in dangerous foreign lands, often losing life or limb. Our schools will seek Soldier Saints as prized guest speakers who worked behind-the-scenes to dismember the fourth beast. Students will be inspired to thrive as warriors and problem solvers in society.

Arts

During the classical period, the arts celebrated the Creator of the universe and the stunning beauty of nature. Under the fourth beast, art diminished to meaningless shapes and sculptures often exuding satanic imagery. School libraries are full of books teaching rebellion among children and glorifying deviant lifestyles. Stories of true heroes of the faith and warrior founding fathers and kings are scrubbed. Popular children's books seek to instill curiosity and interest in witchcraft and the occult. Porn and alternative lifestyle books exist in nearly every public-school library in the United States.

When the power of the fourth beast breaks, the classical arts will return. A new generation of inspired artists will emerge, illustrating stories of men and women transformed and healed by the glory of God in miraculous ways. Our society, repulsed and utterly embarrassed by the brainwashing endured under the fourth beast, will flock to the truth and purity of God's Word.

Religion

Sadly, the Church encouraged infiltration by the fourth beast. Many Christian denominations compromised to the point where they embrace gay marriage and other alternative lifestyles. Many Christian churches today lack the power to help people overcome temptation. Some churches preach godly living, but they lack the knowledge or power to help people live a godly lifestyle and get free. Suffering from rapture paralysis, many pastors don't speak the truth because they possess a fatalistic view that conditions progressively worsen before the rescue rapture. The vast majority of churches today rely on secular social media platforms, causing some pastors to shy from the truth for fear of attracting enough attention to get deplatformed by monopolistic tech executives.

The fourth beast declared war on the American Church. In a brilliant control ploy, the IRS routinely threatens to pull the 501c3 exemption status of churches that engage in political discourse. U.S. churches are now threatened that they must accept LGBTQ leaders into their midst, despite religious convictions to the contrary. As a result, many pastors stay out of the political fray and Sunday services don't arm church members to fight for Christian values. The rest of the week church members keep their heads down. In China and other parts of the world, Christian persecution reaches unprecedented levels.

When the fourth beast dies, the true Church will regain its platform and provide leadership in the seven pillars of society. A great exposure and cleansing will occur within the Church. Many pastors will be restored to their first love of Jesus and publicly repent for allowing their churches to compromise. Unrepentant pastors that participated and profited from the fourth beast system will be judged.

The coming revival, complete with the tangible and visible glory of God, will cause church attendance to swell. The coming revival will occur despite the Church leadership. Ordinary, untrained Christians who simply cried out for a move of God led powerful and incredible revivals in the past. Revivals cause a leadership shift in the Church – ordinary people without seminary degrees step up to lead. The next move of God will likely be lay led. My own story provides a great example. I gained insight into the Kingdom Age of the Saints not from a seminary or even from my pastor. I did not earn a seminary degree. The Kingdom Age of the Saints insight came to me by the Holy Spirit after months of crying out to God for answers to questions regarding the End Times and how to properly care for my family.

The world's welfare system belongs to the Church, not godless governments. The Church is commanded to take care of widows, orphans, poor people, and the hungry with generosity. With additional resources available to the saints, an incredible abundance of goods exists for the needy. James 1:27 (NLT) states, "Pure and genuine religion in the sight of God the Father means caring for the orphans and widows in their distress and refusing to let the world corrupt you." Our duty as the Church includes taking care of people in need worldwide. God did not create the earth without the resources needed to supply His prized creation, people. In fact, in Genesis 1:28 (KJV) God gave humans a combination blessing and command, "Be fruitful, and multiply, and replenish the earth, and subdue it." The scarcity concept is satanic and the opposite of what the Bible says. The Church's incredible generosity and love will draw many into the Church.

A few years ago I accepted the invitation to visit the Green family in Oklahoma as part of a group. David Green, CEO of Hobby Lobby Stores, outlined his family's vision of using their business profits to further the gospel. Each year, through the Hobby Lobby enterprise, hundreds of millions of dollars in profit are generated. The Green family funnels these profits into evangelistic ministries bringing people to Christ. During my visit I felt God's desire for many more families like the Greens. Other successful entrepreneurs have demonstrated a missionary mindset, such as R. G. LeTourneau, a sixth-grade dropout who later ranked among the top government contractors in World War II, primarily for his massive earthmoving equipment and services. LeTourneau used his business profits and roadbuilding equipment to evangelize Latin America and other continents in the 1940s and 1950s. He later endowed a Christian university in Longview, Texas.[105] When God prospers His true saints, good things happen and society benefits.

God will raise many new billionaires who care for humanity and are passionate about leading people to Jesus. Upon the removal of powerful monopolistic barriers of the fourth beast, many saints will prosper and do well. More Christian millionaires and billionaires will thrive than at any other time in history. Allow God to expand your vision in your own life and do not fear.

---

[105] R. G. LeTourneau, *Mover of Men and Mountains: The Autobiography of R. G. LeTourneau* (Chicago: Moody Press, 1967).

"When the saints rule the world during the Kingdom Age of the Saints, Satan still roams. For this reason, God will entrust only saints who are wise as serpents to lead. Too many saints are easily deceived and naive. Now is the time to wake up to the enemies devices and learn to hear and recognize God's voice. Cut off the mainstream news and distraction and learn to speak with God."

– Benjamin Thomas

11. The Rapture and the Dragon

The Angel said to me, "Write this: Blessed are those invited to the Wedding Supper of the Lamb." He added, "These are the true words of God!

– Rev 19:9 MSG

After the death of the fourth beast, the saints exercise geopolitical dominion on earth for a long time. I believe the age of freedom lasts several hundred years, during the time that the sixth seal opens in Revelation 6. The Kingdom Age of the Saints produces an unprecedented time of peace and spiritual revival. The saints are in authority, and the former elites aligned with the fourth beast go into hiding. At the end of the time of the sixth seal, 144,000 people of original Judean-Israel origin, a type of Soldier Saint, emerges to do battle with the dragon, otherwise known as the anti-Christ, by evangelizing new Christian converts in the time of tribulation. At this point, the saints of God are called to heaven for the great gala after a glorious rapture event. Reunited with His Church, Jesus treats His saints to a great celebration (Rev 19:6-9), commonly described as the marriage supper of the Lamb. Upon the opening of the seventh seal in Revelation 6, all hell breaks loose and an unprecedented time of intense tribulation on earth begins, led by a dangerous fifth beast, also referred to as the dragon or the anti-Christ.

In Matthew 25, Jesus lays out powerful parables to help us prepare for the Kingdom Age of the Saints, and the marriage supper that follows. The first parable describes ten virgins all waiting for a special marriage feast, the marriage supper of the Lamb. Five prepare by keeping their oil full, five fail – 50 percent fall away. The parable of the virgins indicates that staying on fire for God requires vigilance during the kingdom age, due to the delay. Jesus then goes on in a subsequent parable to describe a time frame in which God gives talents (money) to saints to produce a return. I believe this parable describes the kingdom age. You see, when the transfer of wealth occurs, God watches what we do with the resource. Will we produce a harvest for God? In Matthew 25:19 (AMPC), the Scripture states, "Now after a long time, the master of those servants returned and settled accounts with them." The long time indicates the time of the Kingdom Age of the Saints, which likely lasts hundreds of years. The talents represent the transfer of wealth which occurs. God expects us to do something with the talents (resources) we receive. The master in the parable provides little to no mentoring to his servants. The master endows gifts according to abilities and then expects a report when he returns. The servants that produce a return are given additional responsibility. The master judges the servant who buries his gift severely. Later in the same chapter, Jesus discusses separating the sheep and goat nations and also takes stock of who fed the hungry, the thirsty, and entertained strangers (vs. 35). You see, the gifts bestowed during the Kingdom Age of the Saints must be put to use. We are to prayerfully seek out our purpose and measure our impact the way that Jesus expects.

Unfulfilled Bible Prophecies for the Church

Many Biblical prophecies must be fulfilled before the tribulation when the anti-Christ rules. I believe the unfulfilled prophecies occur during the Kingdom Age of the Saints. The whole world must be evangelized (Mark 13:10). Every person on earth must hear the redeeming message of Jesus and be provided an opportunity to accept Him. Some experts believe the whole earth will hear the gospel of Jesus Christ by AD 2033.[106] The excellent work of Christian missionaries and Bible translators ensures the fulfillment of Mark 13:10 in just a few years. Although the nation of Israel exists, the temple needs to be rebuilt to allow for the resumption of animal sacrifices, according to the law of Moses (Dan. 9:27). Another important milestone includes the Church achieving a state of perfection. Jesus presents to Himself a church without spot or blemish (Eph. 5:27). A church infiltrated by the fourth beast, including the long-subdued and corrupt Vatican, hardly represents a body without spot or blemish. And Christians hiding from Satan, cowering in fear of the fourth beast, do not represent a perfect church. The fourth beast's death paves the way for cleansing and empowering the Church before the Lord returns for His bride.

An oft-overlooked sign includes God's glory filling the earth (Num. 14:21; Hab. 2:14; Isa. 11:9; Rev 18:1). Some scholars argue

---

[106] "Why Audio?" *Faith Comes by Hearing*, accessed June 23, 2023, https://www.faithcomesbyhearing.com.

this sign is reserved for the millennial reign of Christ, but I believe the tangible glory assists the saints in gathering many to God as well as serves to purify the Church during the Kingdom Age of the Saints. We saw glimpses during famous revivals where the tangible glory of God appeared, such as the New York City revival of 1857, the Azusa Street revival in 1906, or the Hebrides revival in 1949. During the ministry of the late Kenneth E. Hagin, the tangible glory of God appeared in certain services. He described this as a mist during which miracles would occur. These occurrences, however, were short-term or appeared in isolation. A day is coming when God's glory fills the earth and major revival breaks out worldwide. The Lord is merciful, and He shows the world His glory to draw in as many followers as possible. Many people professing to be Jews will accept Jesus as Messiah. During this time, any person not attracted to the Lord's glory and to repentance will likely not repent during the time of the dragon. This may explain why a messianic evangelistic team of only 144,000 suffices during the Great Tribulation.

The Anti-Christ Can't Come While We're Here

Because of the spiritual authority of believers, Christians must be raptured before the anti-Christ exercises complete rule. Christians who know how to exercise their authority using the name of Jesus wield profound force over the demonic principalities on earth (Luke 10:19). When Jesus walked the earth, He exercised dominion over Satan by regularly casting out demons and healing the sick. He commanded His disciples and other followers to do the same. Today many ministries train their people to successfully deal with demonic possession and disease. Prophets in the Old Testament regularly judged the kings of the earth and disrupted the best-laid secular battle plans. God did not change – the same prophetic ministry exists today.

Modern-day prophets such as the late Kim Clement and Robin Bullock issue prophetic warnings to various political leaders around the world, literally thwarting the enemy's plans and showing us glimpses of how God sees the world today. What's more, Christian intercessors worldwide pull down strongholds and use the name of Jesus in powerful, effective prayer. The anti-Christ can't operate and exercise virtually unlimited power on the earth while the prayer warriors and mighty prophets are exercising their spiritual authority. Second Thessalonians 2:7 (NCV) supports this: "The secret power of evil is already working in the world, but there is one who is stopping that power. And he will continue to stop it until he [the Church] is taken out of the way." The fourth beast's attempts to bring in the dragon (or anti-Christ) before his time are thwarted by the praying saints and prophets holding him back.

The Great Tribulation

When Christians unite with the Lord during the marriage supper of the Lamb, great darkness returns to earth for a brief period, commonly referred to as the Great Tribulation (see Fig. 5). The fourth beast will revive in the form of the anti-Christ (also referred to as the dragon). The descendants of the families once ruling during the time of the fourth beast will gleefully come out of hiding and retake leadership positions over the seven pillars of society. For power transfer to happen quickly, the considerable wealth possessed by the saints who ruled during the kingdom age likely transfers to the demonic agents of the anti-Christ. Armed with worldly wealth and unhindered by prayer warriors, the anti-Christ possesses virtually unfettered power. The anti-Christ rules the earth for a relatively short time. Based on Daniel 9:27, many scholars believe the anti-Christ rules for seven years.

Figure 5 shows the sequence of events after the stone judgment. For a more detailed depiction showing the timeline and other information, visit revelationriddle.com.

Figure 5: *Biblical Sequence Following the Stone Judgment*

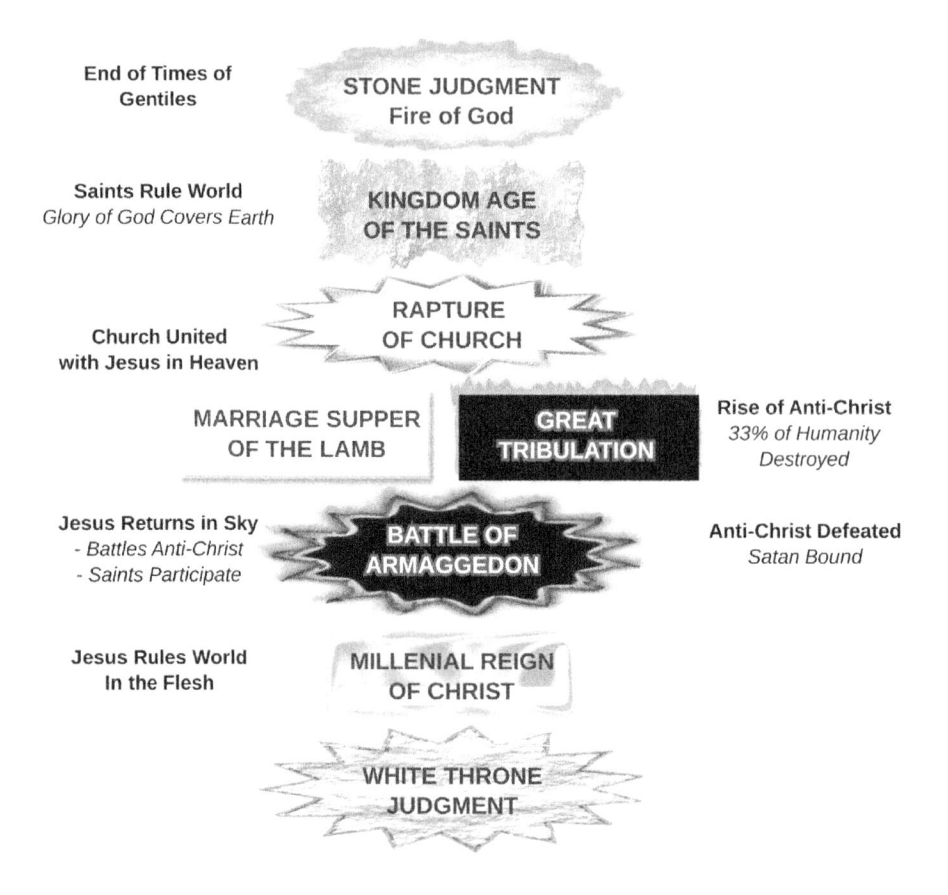

End of Times of Gentiles	STONE JUDGMENT — Fire of God	
Saints Rule World — Glory of God Covers Earth	KINGDOM AGE OF THE SAINTS	
Church United with Jesus in Heaven	RAPTURE OF CHURCH	
	MARRIAGE SUPPER OF THE LAMB / GREAT TRIBULATION	Rise of Anti-Christ — 33% of Humanity Destroyed
Jesus Returns in Sky — Battles Anti-Christ — Saints Participate	BATTLE OF ARMAGGEDON	Anti-Christ Defeated — Satan Bound
Jesus Rules World In the Flesh	MILLENIAL REIGN OF CHRIST	
	WHITE THRONE JUDGMENT	

Revelation 17:8 (KJV) describes the fourth beast as one that "*was, and is not; and shall ascend out of the bottomless pit,* and go into perdition" (emphasis added). The passage points to the death

of the fourth beast and subsequent reemergence as a dragon at a later point, who resurrects the image of the fourth beast. Revelation 13:11-12 (ASV) says, "I saw another beast coming up out of the earth; and he had two horns like unto a lamb, and he spake as a dragon. And he exerciseth all the authority of the first beast in his sight. And he maketh the earth and them that dwell therein to worship the first beast, whose death-stroke was healed." The dragon, *the fifth beast*, brings back the image of the fourth beast and once again dominates the earth with tighter control over society and more destructive ability than the fourth beast. For instance, while the fourth beast kills about 25 percent of humanity (already fulfilled), an additional one-third of humanity dies during the time of the dragon.

The dragon institutes and enforces a mark, required to buy and sell goods. According to Revelation 13:16-17, "he causeth all, the small and the great, and the rich and the poor, and the free and the bond, that there shall be given them a mark on their right hand, or upon their forehead; and that no man should be able to buy or to sell, save he that hath the mark." The dragon causes those who don't receive the mark or worship the beast to be executed. The current fourth beast operates behind the curtain of governments and finance. However, the dragon will travel with a famous false prophet who performs great signs, such as calling down fire from heaven (Rev 19:20). The signs performed by the false prophet are convincing; after observing the signs, many on the earth believe the dragon worthy of worship. Unlike the fourth beast, who rules in an obscure way with a league of nations exercising the authority of a mysterious little horn, the dragon is a visible, demanding leader seeking direct worship.

What the fourth beast failed to accomplish despite best efforts at CERN, the dragon accomplishes. The bottomless pit opens and demonic spirits are unleashed on the population such as the world has never seen (Rev 9:3). Before the tribulation, God exposes His glory to the world during a great spiritual outpouring. Those who still reject the Lord readily accept the mark of the dragon. As a result, they are incredibly susceptible with no defense from demonic possession. Demon-possessed people will wander the streets like zombies, in absolute torment, with precious few exorcists to help them or provide relief.

The dragon's enormous military army numbers 200 million (Rev 9:16). His army terrorizes anyone who does not worship the dragon and penalizes nations failing to submit or yield their authority to the dragon. The dragon uses the technology infrastructure already in place along with new advances during the Kingdom Age of the Saints to provide surveillance on everyone on earth. Remember, Satan is not the Holy Spirit; he needs human technology to observe people and understand what they are doing. Satan needs computers, AI, and machine learning to effect his control. Today, we see signs of surveillance technology in action, but it's a dry run. Technological tools are weaponized and fully employed when the dragon assumes power.

The 144,000: A Thorn in the Side of the Anti-Christ

I believe the 144,000 elect who refuse the dragon's mark are Judean converts who recognize Jesus as Messiah shortly after the Rapture. This group is special in the eyes of God. These virgins, blameless in the sight of God, learn a heavenly song that no one else could learn to sing (Rev 14:3-4). Perhaps this song represents code to help the elect evade the surveillance techniques of the dragon. I believe these people cause many to recognize Jesus as Messiah and Savior during the Great Tribulation – a time of great Jewish messianic conversion and revival. While the converts will take great risks and likely lose their lives, heaven welcomes them. In God's great mercy, He will continue to give people chances to accept Him, even employing an angel to share the gospel (Rev 14:6). In *Left Behind: The Rise of the Antichrist*, a movie starring Kirk Cameron, angels evangelize through a rogue missionary group who takes over the anti-Christ's news media station for a brief moment to share the gospel message and compel people to repent.[107] Regardless of God's method, He shows His mercy even during the most difficult time on earth.

Armageddon: Short and Sweet

The anti-Christ's reign ends during the battle of Armageddon, when Jesus returns in the sky and confronts the dragon – overcoming him in a victorious battle. The short battle delivers a clear and decisive victory over the dragon (Rev 19:20). The dragon's army is consumed on the battlefield (v. 21). Jesus then binds the dragon for a thousand years (Rev 20:3). The saints return to earth, and Jesus rules in the flesh on earth during the thousand-year term of the millennial reign of Christ.

Millennial Reign of Christ

Revelation 20:1-3 (MSG) describes the millennial reign of Christ. Satan is bound and no longer able to deceive the nations:

> I saw an Angel descending out of Heaven. He carried the key to the Abyss and a chain – a huge chain. He

---

[107] *Left Behind: The Rise of the Antichrist*, dir. Kevin Sorbo, prod. Paul LaLonde et al., 2023.

grabbed the Dragon, that old Snake – the very Devil, Satan himself! – chained him up for a thousand years, dumped him into the Abyss, slammed it shut and sealed it tight. No more trouble out of him, deceiving the nations – until the thousand years are up. After that he has to be let loose briefly.

Daniel 7:13-14 (ASV) foretells the glorious age when Jesus reigns and all people serve Him as the visible King:

> I saw in the night-visions, and, behold, there came with the clouds of heaven one like unto a son of man, and he came even to the ancient of days, and they brought him near before him. And there was given him dominion, and glory, and a kingdom, that all people, nations, and languages should serve him: his dominion is an everlasting dominion, which shall not pass away, and his kingdom that which shall not be destroyed.

During the future age when Jesus reigns physically, all people serve our Lord, and Satan is locked away. Biblical scholars refer to the future age as the millennial reign of Christ. During this age, evil people are not hiding in caves waiting for the dragon to restore their power! What Daniel sees in his vision is the time when Jesus comes to establish His kingdom on the earth, ruling in the flesh. Daniel 7:27 (Darby) speaks to both ages – the Kingdom Age of the Saints, who lead by the Holy Spirit, and the millennial reign of Christ, where Jesus, the King of kings rules in the flesh:

> But the kingdom and the dominion, and the greatness of the kingdoms under the whole heavens, shall be given

to the people of the saints of the most high [places]. His kingdom is an everlasting kingdom, and all dominions shall serve and obey him.

God's plan all along included elevating His people to leadership positions, empowered and purified by His glory, to bring on a time of great harvest in the earth. Satan's efforts to tamp down the Church and stifle the glory fail. In fact, with the glory comes God's goodness, and a population explosion occurs simultaneously with a great harvest of souls. We fulfill the blessed command and promise of Genesis 1:28. You see, God promised His glory would fill the earth. His people carry the glory. Listen to Daniel 12:3 (AMPC), "And the teachers and those who are wise shall shine like the brightness of the firmament, and those who turn many to righteousness (to uprightness and right standing with God) [shall give forth light] like the stars forever and ever." Daniel 12 discusses God's people shining brightly and bringing many to righteousness. Some people say this verse refers to the millennial reign of Christ. However, why would we need to turn people to righteousness during the millennial reign, when Satan is bound? People also get confused with words like forever. Keep in mind that once the fourth beast is slain, God's people never again are under the thumb of satanic rule. Jesus calls His Church to the marriage supper before Satan again rules the world under the dragon, the anti-Christ. God's plan is *so much better* than we were taught. Are you ready, Soldier Saints? God's judgment comes for the fourth beast. For the Church, it appears as glory and power.

The heaven, even the heavens, are the Lord's: but the earth hath he given to the children of men.

– Ps. 115:16 KJV

12. Prepare, Soldier Saints!

God blessed them and said, Have many children and grow in number. Fill the earth and be its master. Rule over the fish in the sea and over the birds in the sky and over every living thing that moves on the earth.
– Gen. 1:28 NCV

The most powerful event since the resurrection of Jesus happens soon. Following the judgment and execution of the fourth beast, the saints inherit geopolitical dominion over the earth. Judgment of the fourth beast begins slowly but then culminates suddenly in a visible manner. Satan's plan to eradicate humanity will fail in front of our eyes. The planet continues to wake up to the fourth beast's lies and deception as plans and players are exposed. The nobles of the earth who participated in the fourth beast system are soon judged and go into hiding. The days of wearing out the saints end forever. Soldier Saints not only help judge the fourth beast but lead the next glorious age. How do we get ready for this?

Adopt Lifestyle of Conversing with God

Getting prepared starts with spiritual health. Begin to detox off of the fourth beast forms of entertainment and fear porn, including mainstream news and talk shows. Spend quality time each day reading the Bible and listening to God. Fast a few meals a week to keep your flesh down. Dedicate the first half hour to an hour of the day worshiping God and reading His Word. Start a prayer journal with two colored pens, one color for your own words and one to record the words of the Holy Spirit. Each day, date your journal and write your thoughts, concerns, and dreams to God. Then spend time quietly waiting for the response from the Holy Spirit – record what He tells you. This simple act puts you in a place of faith and expectation. Jesus promises to speak to us: "My sheep hear my voice" (John 10:27 KJV). He also promises that the Holy Spirit will guide us into all the truth and show us things to come (John 16:13). Powerful promises regarding hearing God's voice are for us today. God still speaks to His people. I am amazed how the Holy Spirit guides me while I am journaling and listening to God.

Decide to eliminate fear from your life. A wise teacher once told me, "Faith and fear take the same energy, each involves believing that what you can't see will come to pass." Don't give fear any energy. Decide no matter what you hear in the news, you simply won't buy into fear. Stop worrying about nuclear war, new pandemics, and the like. Fearmongering is a tool the fourth beast uses to keep saints paralyzed and ineffective. We must stop fearing the fourth beast – his days are numbered and his power waning. As part of the fourth beast death gurgle, we likely will observe a few more gasps and scare events, but it's just a matter of time before the fourth beast dies.

Build Up Your Faith

It's hard to talk yourself into faith, especially without God's Word deeply rooted inside of you. The best way to grow your faith is by spending time reading the Scriptures out loud so your ears can hear what you say. Spend a few months simply reading the words of Jesus, which are so encouraging and full of power! If you start to feel fear gripping your heart, recall the promises in the Bible, and don't let go. If you have children, spend time with them reading the Bible and praying together. Married couples should begin praying together, seeking to discover their family's role in the upcoming transition to the Kingdom Age of the Saints.

I got frustrated by the recent Covid lockdowns and began to bitterly complain about them to others. As a frequent traveler the restriction on various national borders annoyed me. One family member would simply say, "Don't worry, I have prayed and by the time my flight happens, there won't be any more restrictions." Sure enough, a few days before their flight, restrictions would drop or something else would happen that would make their trip work after all. This childlike faith humbled me. Instead of complaining about the problem, they dealt with the problem by faith and prayer.

Committing to tackling issues with prayer and faith should be our commitment going forward. Begin to speak to the mountain and expect it to move, through faith in Jesus' name (Mark 11:23).

Apply the Blood of Jesus to Your Family

Before the exodus of Israel from Egypt, God sent a total of ten plagues upon the Egyptians to force their hand to let Israel go. The toughest plague of all, the tenth and final plague, killed the firstborn of each household in Egypt, including Pharaoh's household. Moses instructed each household of Israel to apply a lamb's blood on their doorpost to keep the death angel from visiting their homes and killing their firstborn children as well (Ex. 11–12). Israel commingled with the Egyptians for over four hundred years and likely adopted some of their satanic practices along the way. The blood represented protection from the death angel.

There are numerous other examples of the blood providing protection in the Old Testament, including the Law of Moses, the story of Rahab (Jericho), and others. Of course, in the New Testament, Christians' sins are wiped away by the blood of Jesus. In Revelation 12:11 (AMPC), the Word states, "They overcame and conquered him [Satan] because of the blood of the Lamb and because of the word of their testimony, for they did not love their life and renounce their faith even when faced with death." How do we apply the blood to our lives? Here's a simple prayer: "Father, I plead the blood of Jesus over my family, and I draw a line of the blood of Jesus around my family, my property, my bank accounts and my possessions, in Jesus' name."

Right now, we are entering the period of the stone judgment. God judges our evil oppressors, and the judgment is not intended for His saints. However, like the children of Israel in the time of judgment of Egypt, we must apply the blood of Jesus in our own lives to avoid getting caught up in the judgment. For more information on this subject, I highly recommend the book *The Blood and the Glory* by Billye Brim.[108] While Ms. Brim and I don't align on all matters related to End Times teaching, she offers amazing insight in her book on applying the blood of Jesus for divine protection, as well as God's desire to share His glory with us.

Discover Your Destiny

God gave every person on earth a destiny and one or more unique gifts to fulfill their destiny. Your gift may include encouraging others or intercessory prayer. My gift involves building successful businesses to enable me to give strategically. I also pray for the sick and am fortunate to witness miracles. Regardless of who you are, you have a special gift related to your destiny. I know of a particular businessman passionate about education, with great ideas to transform our educational system. He started his microschool in California and hired teachers to teach the kids in the neighborhood for a couple of years. This gentleman acted after recognizing a problem with the quality of local schools. He later took his ideas to Turning Point USA, and now an entire team is working on transforming the education system. Despite humble beginnings, this team of saints may end up serving as the new leadership in the U.S. school system after the fall of the fourth beast. One frustrated parent in California decided to *do something*, and now a powerful team is assembled and ready to go when the opportunity arises.

    I firmly believe God already began assembling His leadership team from among the saints to lead the next age. If you want to be

---
[108] Billye Brim, *The Blood and the Glory* (Tulsa, OK: Harrison House, 1995).

part of the new leadership team, start moving out with your gifts and passions and you will be amazed at how quickly things can come together. As we approach the Kingdom Age of the Saints, time is accelerating. Dreams are accomplished at lightning speed.

      Your gift from God is your potential. Your gift to God is living up to your potential. Don't neglect your gift because you believe the rescue rapture is soon coming to take you to heaven. Stop waiting to see what happens. Begin to move out in faith in an area that interests you. Take a first step of faith, and then watch God provide the resources you need. Length of life is not measured solely by years; it's also measured by breadth. How wide are you living your life? Are you advancing in the knowledge of faith? Soldier Saints know their purpose and move out in faith to pursue their purpose. This may or may not be visible to others.

Cancel Culture: Ignore It

I know some people who get in their prayer closet daily to pray for their country and leaders – Soldier Saints operating in the spirit realm. Other Soldier Saints are using their platform to stand up to tyranny. The fourth beast's voice, the media, frequently trolls these Soldier Saints, and many have suffered relational loss with friends and family members as a result. Soldier Saints are not popular with the world. I spoke to a Soldier Saint recently who apologized to me about the negative press that they received for standing up to communist curriculum seeking to make its way into the classroom in their respective state. My perspective is that negative press is a badge of honor in many cases. A common tactic of the fourth beast includes vilifying effective leaders in an attempt to shut them down. Don't let it get to you. You are in good company with other Soldier

Saints who experienced the same treatment. Throughout the Bible we see similar examples. The "press" vilified Noah, Gideon, King David, Nehemiah, Jonah, Jesus, the disciples, and countless others. The enemy fears even a single obedient Soldier Saint operating within their calling. Remember Sean Feucht, who decided to stand up to the Covid tyranny and worship God on a bridge in San Francisco. Unfortunately, the Church stood in line first to vilify Sean. Who was right in the end?

What if Money Were No Object?

Begin to imagine a life, purpose, and ministry where money no longer serves as a barrier. What would you do, for instance, with access to unlimited funds? How would you help restore humanity after millennia of oppression by the fourth beast? Which cause excites you? If nothing comes to mind, begin to seek a higher purpose from God. Ask yourself, "Am I a generous person?" If you are not a regular tither to your local church, pursue obedience regarding your giving. Obedience in giving unlocks favor from God. If God cannot trust us with our giving, He won't bless us with additional resources. Second Corinthians 9:6, says "[Remember] this: he who sows sparingly and grudgingly will also reap sparingly and grudgingly, and he who sows generously [that blessings may come to someone] will also reap generously and with blessings."

While funds and the transfer of wealth flow to all saints after the death of the fourth beast, the generous and faithful reap exceptional rewards and favor, including generational wealth. Ask God to use you in this manner and be prepared for almost immediate direction to bless others. Cain failed to please God not because Cain farmed and his brother, Abel, raised sheep. In Genesis 4:3,

Cain brought his offering over a period of time. In other words, Cain dragged his feet on the offering, after the plants wilted. Abel, on the other hand, brought the first fruits, the best sheep, to God. Learn to be quick to obey.

Stewardship is the Key

God teaches stewardship throughout the Bible. The Israelites repeatedly failed the stewardship test. God delivered them from bondage to Egypt and equipped them with wealth, and they tested Him by complaining, doubting, and building idols of foreign gods. These stories serve to warn the saints of the same folly. When asset pools of the wicked are distributed to the saints, we will come into massive wealth. Wealth is an amplifier of both good and evil. A pure heart immediately focuses on blessing others. An evil heart seeks to hoard and steal from others. Intentionality starts in obedience with the resources we possess today, such as tithing to a local church and helping needy people around us. However, true elevation involves writing plans to bless others when resources come. Years ago, a financial distribution from a business I sold got delayed. The Lord dealt with me to pray and come up with a giving plan. I spent weeks praying over amounts for ministries and other organizations I planned to bless once the financial distribution happened. Having agreed on the specific amounts, I transferred the illiquid assets to the targeted organizations in an act of faith. When the financial distribution came, many organizations benefited. Intentionality and prayerful planning prepared my heart to receive blessings from God. I also believe it unlocked the delay.

In an exercise of faith, construct a humanitarian plan to exercise upon receipt of wealth. I am not saying that wealth should not also take care of your family, provide college funds for your children, and so on. However, "The generous will prosper; those who refresh others will themselves be refreshed" (Prov 11:25 NLT). God cares not whether His people possess money; He does not want money to possess His people. The fourth beast erred greatly by hoarding technologies, resources, and great wealth for itself, designing systems to suck the resources from others simply to amass large asset pools. The extreme selfishness and greed of the fourth beast, satanic in nature, robbed humanity for thousands of years. God expects more from His saints.

Beginning with my lawn mowing business during my teens, I knew to tithe the first 10 percent or more of my income to my local church. I found the secret – the 90 percent remaining after the tithe goes further than the 100 percent because of God's heavenly covenant. The only Scripture where God openly challenges men and women to prove Him relates to the covenant of giving. Malachi 3:10 (AMPC) states, "Bring all the tithes (the whole tenth of your income) into the storehouse, that there may be food in My house, and prove Me now by it, says the Lord of hosts, if I will not open the windows of heaven for you and pour you out a blessing, that there shall not be room enough to receive it." The Scripture in Malachi followed a rebuke to Israel regarding their giving (or lack thereof).

Tithing and giving not only funds the Church but represents obedience, qualifying saints for God's unlimited blessings. In the last few years, I have prayed about every giving opportunity, and I give amounts God shows me at the time. In annual accounting I notice the percentage is typically higher than the requisite 10 percent. Giving takes obedience and patience. You may be challenged to give to someone in need something you value greatly. Practice fast obedience; don't think twice. God always makes it up to you by multiplying the seeds you sow.

The Church Is Confused Regarding Wealth

Confusion abounds in the Church regarding giving and wealth. Many Christians recall the story where Jesus asks the rich young ruler to give his wealth to the poor and follow Him. They point to this as proof that God does not want His people to prosper financially. Thousands of verses in the Bible point to financial stewardship and the blessing that follows. The rich young ruler failed to understand that if Jesus asked him to sow his wealth, He would make it up to him. Jesus lovingly tried to break the young ruler's bondage of faith in money and extended an invitation to him to join Jesus' ministry. Had the young ruler obeyed Jesus' command, I am certain that even greater and unexpected material wealth would follow. In the event the young ruler joined Jesus as a ministry disciple, then a specific high calling rested on the young ruler far exceeding the gift of strategic giving.

Listen to Matthew 19:29 (MSG): "Anyone who sacrifices home, family, fields – whatever – because of me will get it all back a hundred times over, not to mention the considerable bonus of eternal life." Christians today don't experience material blessings because they fail to consider their part in the equation. We must first prove ourselves generous and obedient givers and then ask God for ways to prosper. Earlier I mentioned R.G. LeTourneau, an extraordinarily wealthy and generous inventor. In his book, LeTourneau details how his heart yearned to support missionaries, and he cried out to God for ideas on how to prosper. God gave

LeTourneau an idea for a tractor with a shovel on the front (the first bulldozer), and the rest is history.

In heaven gold is used in place of asphalt to pave streets. God's extravagance represents His generous nature. It's up to us to get our hearts right so we are in a place to receive. To truly qualify for abundance, start seeing money as a tool to bless others and your work as a means to bless others.

NEVER Take Off God's Armor

The apostle Paul exhorts the saints, "Put on God's whole armor [the armor of a heavy-armed soldier which God supplies], that you may be able successfully to stand up against [all] the strategies and deceits of the devil" (Eph. 6:11 AMPC). Paul then goes on to teach us about the armor. Remember that the fourth beast first slowly moves toward death, then suddenly dies. We, the Soldier Saints, possess a role in bringing the fourth beast down. Without fully donning the armor of God, we are ineffective in battle. Our weapon, the sword, is the Word of God. Begin to discover God's promises in Scripture and speak them over various situations. Daily, I declare the Word over my city and country and also thank God for protecting Soldier Saints on the front line of the battle.

Soldiers *never* remove their breastplates in battle, the most important piece of personal armor that guards vital organs. Christians need to keep on the breastplate of righteousness by acknowledging that Jesus fully paid the price for our righteousness – we can't earn it on our own. Our shield, which repels attacks from the enemy, should be large enough to cover our body. Paul teaches us our shield is faith. Faith comes by hearing the Word of God (Rom.

10:17). Lack of a steady diet of the nourishing, faith-building Word renders our shield too small and susceptible to attacks. If even a day or two goes by when I fail to feed on God's Word, I find myself susceptible to fear, dismay, and hopelessness. We must keep strong in the Word and recognize it is not *our* armor we wear but *God's*. When we go into the battle, the enemy sees a bright figure coming toward him that looks like God, and he's very afraid. What would life be like if you knew you would never lose a battle? When we go to battle wearing God's armor, we can't lose. We will be persecuted, for sure. However, even in death, we win.

Those who have played football know how to keep their feet moving to avoid getting knocked off balance. Soldier Saints keep their feet moving. When they see a problem, they work to fix it. Recently, I attended a conference sponsored by the Great Awakening Project. Several Soldier Saints presented how they are impacting their communities and turning things around. I distinctly remember a panel where one saint was taking on election fraud, another battling sinister education agendas, and another rebuilding school boards with highly qualified candidates. Another Soldier Saint team focused on turning around cities and showing excellent results. Several in the room aspired to hold public office, and a few currently serve. When we pray for God to use us, He typically gives us simple things we can do in our community or sphere of influence and provides us with the resources to do so. Yes, we may face challenges and persecution. However, if we want a better world for our children, it's worth it. In Eric Metaxas's book *Letter to the American Church*,[109] he encourages the Church to stand up to tyranny. Many do not. I believe now is the testing ground by God as He

---

[109] Eric Metaxes, *Letter to the American Church* (Salem Books, 2022).

handpicks the team to lead the Kingdom Age of the Saints. Right now, Christians are in the interview process. God is looking for strong men and women to lead and is presently looking at our resumes.

Now's Not the Time to Hide Our Talents

I bear bad news for the saints hiding out in a figurative cave, waiting for the rescue rapture. You won't be used by God to your full potential during the kingdom age. Unless you start using your gifts to help others, you don't qualify. You bought into the fear and don't understand God's plan for humanity. It is for you that I wrote this book. Some preparation for a bumpy transition is fine. Investing in defensive assets such as gold and silver and having cash and other supplies on hand is smart. Just don't bury your talents in the ground, so to speak (see Matt. 25:14-30). When the fourth beast is slain, confused and disoriented people need your gift and counseling to get through it. Remember that a small fraction of the population directly leads the fourth beast system. The vast majority don't have anything to do with it and are just trying to get by. When the fourth beast is judged and faith in humanity is shaken, people desperately need to learn about Jesus (if they don't already know Him). Millions of Christians dulled to the slow and steady brainwashing of the fourth beast will need heartfelt, sincere counseling.

Time to Reboot the Planet

Proverbs 29:2 (NLT) says, "When the godly are in authority, the people rejoice. But when the wicked are in power, they groan." When the saints rule the planet, a massive, joyful revival will break out. As people realize the extent of the satanic evil that existed among the previous world leadership, most will be repulsed and confused. They will not know what to do next and will seek God's plan for their life. God's goodness will draw people in, and He will unleash His glory on the earth. This is the revival we pray for – worldwide in scope and a celebration of God's goodness.

Rebuilding our society on the firm foundation of God's Word happens next: the planet rebooted with a different operating system. A few of the fourth beast handlers will linger, forced to shrink into the woodwork, defeated and demoralized. The dethroned fourth beast workers are not able to comprehend the spiritual awakening in the land. The surviving fourth beast workers are repulsed by the saints. The fourth beast workers, scammed by the lies of Satan and his henchman, suffer depression and anxiety. Satan is a liar and the author of all lies; all who trusted in him are sorely let down. My prayer is a change of heart brings many to the winning team.

Upon the fourth beast's death, we will embark on our new adventure. A new world awaits – a world without the oppressive control of the fourth beast – ruled by good people. I hope understanding the coming Kingdom Age of the Saints gives you confidence and a fresh perspective. What will your role be in the coming kingdom age? God wants you to know your calling. This I know, "Ask, and God will give to you. Search, and you will find. Knock, and the door will open for you" (Matt. 7:7 NCV).

Through His Word the Lord continues to provide new insights concerning the Kingdom Age of the Saints. For instance, the Lord has special plans for Israel in the kingdom age – He did not forget His covenant with Abraham. As I learn more, I plan to share my insights. I encourage you to search the Scriptures yourself. Hold your head high – we are on the winning side. Check out the study guide to accompany this book – it contains practical tools to prepare for the Kingdom Age of the Saints. Finally, visit revelationriddle.com to access special content. Today is not the End Times for the Church, but it's the End Times for the New World Order and the glorious age before rapture. God's mighty anointing is always very near.

> *He stretched out his hand over the sea, he shook the kingdoms: The Lord hath given a commandment against the merchant city, to destroy the strong holds thereof.*
> *– Isa. 23:11 KJV*

"Serving God is an adventure if you will let Him be Lord. He gives His servants assignments of ever increasing importance as we demonstrate obedience. As I have gotten to know God, I realize He's funny, loving, and wants us to enjoy life. He speaks to us in a language we understand, like a good friend. It's the joy of the Lord that is our strength."

– Benjamin Thomas

Appendix

Don't Wait, Receive Jesus Today!

So you will be saved, if you honestly say, "Jesus is Lord," and if you believe with all your heart that God raised him from death. God will accept you and save you, if you truly believe this and tell it to others.
— *Rom. 10:9-10 CEV*

In the book, I talk about the judgment of God falling on the earth. This judgment is not for God's people, but for the world and people that reject God. It is an especially important time to know God and be close to Him. Don't wait, receive Jesus today!

God wants a relationship with you. Not only that, God has a plan and destiny for your life. To have a relationship with God, we must accept Jesus as our Savior and Lord. You see, sin separates us from God, and we must accept Jesus as Savior to allow His blood to wash away our sins and make our spirits white and pure. This is the first step on our adventure with God.

Receiving Jesus as Lord starts with a prayer that acknowledges our sin and asks Him to wash us clean and accept His sacrifice on the cross for us. Nothing you have done in your past is too big for God's forgiveness. Jesus paid the ultimate price so that we would not have to. But we must, by faith, believe in our hearts and say out loud a prayer of Salvation. Ready? Say this:

> "Dear Lord Jesus, I need you. Come into my life, wash me clean. Set me free from all bondage. Heal my body, mind and spirit. Wash me with your blood and protect me with your blood going forward. Fill me with your

Holy Spirit. You are you my Lord and Savior. Give me the strength to serve you all my days."

Find a local church that believes in the miracles of God. Get a Bible and ask God to show you how to read it. Tell others what happened to you. After your decision to serve the Lord, pressure may arise that causes you to doubt. Don't worry about this, it's normal. Satan tries to steal God's Word out of your heart (see Mark 4). Stay close to God through prayer. Talk to God the way you would talk to a close friend, you will soon recognize His voice. He loves you so much, and wants only the best for you.

Printed in Great Britain
by Amazon